May we never
forget !

What readers are saying about
STAIRWELL TO HEAVEN

"A first-hand account of the highest order. To the survivors—all of us—it is a stunning gift of a shared experience. To those who were lost, it is a promise that we will never forget them."

—THOMAS VON ESSEN, *Former Commissioner, FDNY*

"One of a kind. The emotional impact of Earl Johnson's story is so powerful that it will leave you full of gratitude for the gift of your own life!"

—BRIAN PETERS, *President and CEO / RBC Dain Rauscher*

"Wow! What began as an ordinary day for Earl and his family turned into the most devastating event of our time. He lived to tell a gripping survivor's tale . . . and it's a fitting memorial to the fallen."

—RICK WHITE, *former U.S. Congressman and technology CEO*

"A book every American wants to read. A powerful story and reminder . . . not to forget 9-11. I was captivated throughout!"

—BOB MOAWAD, *Chairman and Founder / Edge Learning Institute*

"Earl and Arlene Johnson share their hearts in this personal memoir about 'more' than just surviving the 51st floor of the World Trade Center. Read *Stairwell to Heaven* today and you will learn how an American family overcame some of life's toughest adversities as well as the importance of never forgetting September 11th."

—PATRICK SNOW, *Bestselling Author of* Creating Your Own Destiny

STAIRWELL TO HEAVEN

STAIRWELL TO HEAVEN

A 9-11 World Trade Center Survivor's
Story of Escape, Heroism . . . and Family

EARL C. JOHNSON

with Arlene R. Johnson

©2005 by Earl C. Johnson and Arlene R. Johnson

Library of Congress Control Number: 2005929219

ISBN-10: 1-890427-93-4
ISBN-13: 978-1890427-93-X

First Edition

09 08 07 06 05 6 5 4 3 2 1

Cover and interior design by Lightbourne, Inc.
Cover photography by Pete Saloutos

Books are available at special discounts for quantity purchases,
sales promotions, premiums and fund raising or educational use.
For details, contact: publisher@stairwelltoheaven.com.

ACKNOWLEDGMENTS

It would be an unforgivable omission to not acknowledge the significant contributions and efforts made by the many talented professionals and loving friends who provided their energy, creativity, support and encouragement to our efforts to tell this story.

First, Patrick Snow, author and coach for his early encouragement, detailed roadmap and constant belief in our mission; D-D Smith who delivered first-cut editing to our rough hewn manuscript and Tim Polk for the polishing touches. Graham Van Dixhorn and Susan Kendrick for their magical wordsmithing and sage advise on gaining attention and acceptance in the market for our work; Pete Saloutos and his professional photography team that captured so perfectly for our cover, the emotion and mood within the Stairwell To Heaven; and the creative team at Lightbourne for assembling the total look and feel of our project in such a clear and compelling way as to completely capture my wildest dreams for this book.

Darryl Worley is in a class all by himself and I am proud to provide the formal acknowledgement as required to include his beautiful work within these pages.

Have you Forgotten?
Words and Music by Darryl Worley and Wynn Varble
© 2003 EMI APRIL MUSIC INC., PITTSBURG LANDING SONGS and WARNER-TAMERLANE PUBLISHING CORP. All Rights for PITTSBURG LANDING SONGS Controlled and Administered by EMI APRIL MUSIC INC. All Rights Reserved / International Copyright Secured / Used by Permission

Anita Hogan at International Artists Management for her patience and kindness in helping a complete stranger make his dream come true.

The Bainbridge Island Fire Department and my fellow Commissioners for their dedication and service to our community.

The list of family members and personal friends who have had a positive impact on our efforts is so numerous that we are reluctant to start listing them out of a fear of leaving someone out. We trust that you know who you are and how much your support and caring means to our family.

CONTENTS

PREFACE

Earl C. Johnson

With the fourth anniversary of September 11, 2001 rapidly approaching, I can now look back on my nearly three-year-old idea to write this book and better understand my initial doubts and lack of clarity as to why I felt compelled to tell my story. My doubts were not so much about whether or not anyone would care, but rather, whether I had enough emotional strength to work through the process, revisit in sufficient detail that day of horror, and more importantly be able to offer readers a coherent, broad context from which to view my experience in a way that would meaningfully touch the lives of others.

I believe that now, after nearly four years, I am ready: ready not just to talk about my exodus from the 51st floor of 1 World Trade Center, as I have done for the past three years to dozens of groups, but ready also to offer a broader context to the impact and meaning of that day in my life and hopefully the lives of not only many Americans, but freedom-loving people throughout the world. I have come to believe in the deepest part of my soul that the tragedy of 9-11 holds a historic promise: a promise I could not have known with such clarity had I not been present that fateful day; a promise to all people, free or not, that we as individuals hold the key to an unlimited power of goodness, and the ability, when combined with a will to act, to triumph not only over those in this world who seek to kill, vanquish and enslave their fellow man, but to win the hearts and minds of the purveyors and practitioners of self doubt, guilt, indifference and political correctness that all too often act as effective forces against the expression and realization of a greater goodness.

The pages ahead are filled with my attempt to clarify, illustrate and expound upon this promise in the context of 9-11 and its impact on my life. This effort would have been impossible without the loving support of my wife Arlene and the three most wonderful children on the planet, Cameron, Alex and Noelle. It was Arlene who carried the burden for my family that Tuesday in September 2001. Without her strength and endless support, this book would not exist. It is as much their story as it is mine.

Arlene R. Johnson

Why write this story almost four years later? Why relive the most horrific day of my family's life? What good could come of this? Why torture myself? Who will read it and why would they want to read it? These are the questions I asked myself for almost four years as I attempted several times on paper and in my head to retell the story, the long version. Verbally, I think my husband and I have told the story, both in the long and short form, dozens if not hundreds of times to friends, family and strangers. Sometimes we told it several times in one day after it first happened. In the beginning we just told it, not really questioning why. Then as the months wore on and people kept asking, we realized that people wanted to know more about that day and, more importantly, wanted to know about our life afterwards. They wanted to know that we were okay, that there was life afterwards and that people survived and lived on. Strangers and friends wanted to touch my whole family, wanted to give support, wanted to reach out; some thought it would be lucky. It was strange yet wonderful. The only other time I experienced this phenomenon was when I was pregnant.

At first we were all in shock and simply went through the motions of everyday life, breathing in and out and holding back the tears as much as possible. As months passed, we realized our lives had changed forever; as much as we wanted to put the events of 9-11 behind us, we knew we never would, and we eventually understood that we did not want to. We came to understand that we were survivors and the family of a survivor and that it was our duty to explain what this meant and to make sure people never forgot what that day meant to our country. So began the balancing act of expressing our feelings, yet protecting our children as much as possible. They had already been through so much. But what if we could help them, show them how much good there is in the world? That would be worthwhile. So here is the story of that fateful day, the day that changed forever not only a country but the world; why we were there on the East Coast on such a day; and later what lessons we learned that changed our lives forever for the better. May we never forget.

CHAPTER 1

Why Me?

I'm sure that a majority, if not all, of the survivors from the WTC have asked themselves this question: why me? Psychologists will tell you that feelings of guilt are often experienced by survivors of events or situations during which others have lost their lives. There was a time in the first weeks and months after 9-11 when I did in fact have this very reaction, but somewhere along the path of personal healing, my mind began to focus not on the narrow black-and-white fact of my survival, but instead on an expanded concept of how I came to find myself there for this event and what that reality will mean to everything still to come in my future. I'm sure that it was at this time when I began to realize that for me, true peace of mind would only come through a willingness to accept the fact that there must be, and I must find, the purpose in my presence there that day.

My adult working life has been based in the banking and brokerage world of Wall Street. Not the "Wall Street" physical address in New York City, but rather the trading and sales floors of regional financial centers, including my home town of Seattle, as well as San Francisco, Los Angeles, Chicago and even Memphis. I worked everywhere and anywhere but New York. This was not by accident. Whenever that "brass ring" job presented itself in New York, I always turned it down and, in many cases, never even sought to pursue it. I'm not sure at the time if I was even aware why, but it just never seemed like the right thing to do.

Growing up in the Seattle suburban communities of Mercer Island and then Bainbridge Island, I was fully infected with an outdoors predisposition. As a youth I enjoyed nature's beauty; evergreen trees and blue inland waters were significant influences on my life. Teenage summers spent working in Alaskan salmon canneries honed my love of the outdoors and imprinted a deep sense of home as a place of towering firs, old growth cedars and miles and miles of saltwater shoreline. As a result, my heart always felt displaced when, during my career's early years, I ventured up and down the west coast and midwest. Eventually, maturity came to the rescue, aided in no small part by my marriage to Arlene in 1985, and we settled comfortably back in the Northwest for good.

For the next fifteen years, we enjoyed the best that life in the Northwest has to offer. We struggled like all young families from time to time, but we never questioned where to live. "Where" is a relative term, as we did move several times around the Puget Sound area, but we never considered for a second the option of a long distance move. Our three children had been born, and we were adamant that this was their home. Then in the year 2000, it took a bizarre combination of events, choices and timing, some in our control and many more not, to even entertain the possibility, let alone the need, to move east to New York or New Jersey.

Like many others in the mid 1990s, I was bitten by the technology bug and ventured into the land of high-tech entrepreneurs to form my own software company, Deposit Software Inc. In hindsight, I suppose I can point to this decision as the first step on the road to my date with destiny in New York on September 11, 2001. Like many small, high-tech startups, the financial landscape changed dramatically in the first quarter of 2000 when the door slammed shut on additional venture capital. This macro level economic shift started a chain reaction of events for my family, employees and investors that ended poorly and left me with a broken dream and a nearly empty pocketbook. For the remaining months of 2000 and into early 2001, I fought to pay my bills, provide for my family and find a job in a deteriorating economy.

Throughout this tumultuous period, Arlene and I were adamant about the need and our desire to remain on Bainbridge Island in the house on the water that we had always dreamed of owning. Not that our home was some new, finely sculpted mansion; it was, in fact, in need of many significant upgrades and basic repairs. But the thought of giving it up was too much for either of us to bear. We had sacrificed so much already that we were loath to let our temporary economic circumstances take our home as well. If there is one common attribute of true Northwesterners, it is the desire to own a piece of waterfront property. So much of what the Northwest has to offer happens right in front of your eyes when seen from the shoreline: boats of all kinds, marine birds and mammals, kids inner tubing and water-skiing and squealing in delight. Oh, and let's not forget the great fishing and crabbing that tastes so much better than the store-bought varieties.

Perhaps most significant to me is the sound of the eagles calling each other from the nearby towering evergreens; they sweep down to the water's surface and snatch a small herring or salmon right in front of your eyes. If you haven't seen this for yourself, you can't believe the majesty and grace of these magnificent birds. For me, they represent the ultimate symbol of freedom and strength found in our people and in our country. Strong and powerful, they ignore the constant harassment of lowly crows and seagulls. Focused resolutely on their feeding mission or flight lesson for their young, they never fail to cause me to pause from whatever I'm doing when they appear. It was this magical place we call home which we were so desperately trying to hold on to in the winter of 2000-2001.

Ultimately, my job search took me to New York City, where my previous sales efforts at Deposit Software had uncovered a handful of firms that had survived and prospered with larger capital bases. After an in-person interview and several helpful phone calls on my behalf from old bond trading friends in San Francisco, one of these, Trade Web LLC, offered me a job, and I began commuting cross-country from Bainbridge Island to the 51st floor of 1 World Trade Center in March 2001.

The Decision to Move

The first month or two of my new, long-distance commuting life was a real roller coaster. On the one hand, I was extremely thankful for the needed cash flow from my work at TradeWeb. On the other hand, I was struggling with the intertwined emotions resulting from a never-before experienced separation from my wife and children, while simultaneously trying to move past the blame game played each night when I found myself 3,000 miles from the ones I loved and needed so much. It was very strange and difficult for me. My family and our home play such a central part of my life that I suppose it was almost like an out-of-body experience. I dealt with it the best I could and found myself putting in longer hours, weekends and late nights to fill the alone hours and to climb the steep learning curve presented at work.

Trips home were initially scheduled every three weeks as I tried to take advantage of the 21-day advanced ticket purchase, but I quickly found that two weeks was a better maximum for both my family and myself. In the process, I soon discovered that this effort, while absolutely mandatory for my survival, was extremely exhausting. On a typical visit home, I would leave work on Friday to catch a 6 p.m. non-stop flight from Newark or JFK to Seattle. The flight lasted about six hours if everything went smoothly. Landing at Seattle-Tacoma International Airport at around 9 p.m. west coast time would put me in downtown Seattle at the Coleman ferry dock waiting for the 9:50 sailing home to Bainbridge Island. The forty-five minute crossings were spent upstairs and outside on the upper deck regardless of the weather, enjoying a cigar, the familiar sights of the receding city landscape and the freedom of movement from the confines of the middle seat for six hours. By the time I actually set foot in the front door, it would be close to 11 p.m. The kids were usually already asleep, so Arlene and I would start talking and catch me up on every-thing happening on the home front. The next thing I knew, it would be 2 a.m., and I would be ready to pass out from a nearly 24-hour day.

Saturday mornings have always been my favorite time with the kids. After lots of hugs, kisses, and many more two-way expressions of "I missed you so much", I would set about making the traditional weekend breakfast of bacon, eggs, hash browns and either French toast or cinnamon rolls. The kids would each share with me the events of the past weeks since my last visit, and I would tell them about what new place or thing I had discovered in the Big Apple. In general, we simply spent the entire day as close to one another as possible. Arlene would usually grab this opportunity for some much-deserved alone time and head out for an afternoon of shopping or a movie. Dinner was out at a favorite spot as often as it was a home affair. On Sunday, we would try to make sure we made it to church and not schedule much else. There was usually some house project that required my attention and, of course, the usual maintenance requirements. I tried to always spend some time with our dogs as well: Shadow, our Alaskan Malamute, and Molly, a younger Golden Retriever we had bought for Noelle on her birthday the previous November. But before long, dinner would be over and it was time for me to be packed and heading for the ferry and airport for the 12:30 a.m. red-eye back to New York and my duties Monday morning at work.

Looking back at this time, I am overwhelmed by the sacrifices my family was forced to make as we attempted to regain our financial footing. The tearful goodbyes and constant struggle to understand why Dad works so far away is difficult for Arlene and I to face even today. It is in this context that after several months of repeating this emotional cycle, we came to the point where we needed to be a united family again. We could decide to move east or to try again to find a new opportunity here at home. Given the reality of the weakening economy at the time, it was almost by default that we chose to move. We simply did not have the financial or emotional strength to do anything else. By late April of 2001, as hard as it was to think about moving away, being employed apart or unemployed together were both options that clearly would not work.

Details, Details, Details

At the departure end of this unwelcome but necessary relocation, we had our hands full. I'm sure many readers can relate through direct experience. In some ways, that simple fact gave us a little more confidence in a successful outcome: at least we weren't the first family to go this route. Still, the list of things to do was long and pretty daunting. Arlene did an amazing job of organizing the effort and keeping things moving; no pun intended. My trips home were little whirlwinds of activities, including three garage sales to lighten the load. After the moving company planner paid us our first visit, Arlene and I both knew that we needed to scale our things back to fit into the customary single long-haul tractor-trailer — there was something about the look on his face after a brief tour of the house. I still chuckle when I think about that.

Various planned home improvement projects were shelved to provide time toward fixing the basics, as the house would be on the market soon. Not everything, however, was planned. I remember a call from Arlene one day at work telling me that part of the ceiling surrounding our fireplace and heating system exhaust flues had cracked and fallen several inches in some places and completely tumbled to the floor in other spots. Suffice it to say that I cursed the architect who incorporates the use of a flat roof into a structure built here in the Pacific Northwest. Our house has both sloped sections and one large flat surface that covers the primary living areas of our dining, living and family rooms. Whether due to lack of maintenance, weather, or just old age, the flat roof needed significant repairs surrounding the chimneys, including sub framing thanks to water rot. $9,000 later, everything was shipshape, including a new torch-down surface over the whole "slope challenged" section. Yikes!!

Another unplanned event was the decision by my parents to move before we left, to Boise, Idaho, where my sister and her family lives. Recent years have had their set of challenges for my folks, primarily on the health front. My Dad is 85 and appears at first glance quite fit, but he is significantly experiencing the loss of his memory and independent coping skills. My Mom has had numerous physical ailments, not the least of which was a pituitary gland tumor that required surgery about five years ago. She too requires increasing daily services. Prior to our decision to move east, they were living in a wonderful retirement home right here on Bainbridge Island. It seemed perfect for them, and they liked the familiarity of living again in the community we shared when I was growing up. I remember that their decision to move came as a real shock to me. For some reason, I hadn't considered the possibility that they would move too. But off they went. In Boise, my sister had found a great facility. It was fairly close to her, and Mom and Dad seemed to settle in without much fuss. I realized later that the move was very unsettling for my Dad, as he had never lived outside Seattle except for a brief period in Alaska during World War II. Like a true Northwesterner, he was lost without a shoreline.

Arlene and I began to develop a workable time frame for the move: we wanted to make sure that school would be out for the summer and that Little League baseball was over for the boys. There was no point making it harder than it was going to be anyway. With the timetable established, it became imperative for me to begin in earnest the process of locating a town, school system, commute and house that would accommodate all of our needs. Coincidentally, at this time I had used up my free stay at the Battery Park corporate condo and needed to secure temporary housing for myself before I even began the search for a home for my family. After much discussion and personal enlightenment, Arlene firmly suggested I give up on the idea of becoming a "roommate" for a female flight crew and find someplace cheap with easy access to public transportation. And so I discovered Bayonne, New Jersey. I secured a local paper and with a little effort found a perfect spot. Well, it was perfect in price, commute, landlord and neighbor. My find was a three-story walk-up with an attic studio, no central air conditioning, and a Nun in the second floor apartment. Perfect. It was small, hot and had a low ceiling. At 6'2", it was the latter "attribute" that got to me the most. But two blocks away was the Light Rail to Liberty State Park and Jersey City, linking to the PATH subway into the Towers or the water taxi across the Hudson to the World Financial Center complex. Like I said, perfect.

I soon discovered that in order to make progress on my assigned explorations, I required a car. Rentals were out of the question, as they were ridiculously expensive. Besides, my own car would give me a basic sense of freedom that I had noticeably lacked during my time in New York. There is nothing like a car to renew one's sense of freedom and provide a familiar, comfortable and affordable way to explore new surroundings. I could see a road trip in my immediate future. Little did I know that it would be the first of four such cross-country trips during 2001.

CHAPTER 2

Road Trip

Not usually one to look at the glass half empty, I started to see the need to get my car to the east coast as more of an adventure rather than a burden. After making some inquires into transport services, I came to the conclusion that for the same or less amount of money, I could use the trip as an educational experience for our son Cameron, who would be turning twelve that year. Arlene and I both felt that Cam could not only use some significant alone time with me, he also needed the opportunity to create some personal buy-in toward making the huge change in environment just as he was about to enter junior high school.

I arrived home from New York in typical cross-country commuter fashion late Friday night on May 11th. After a whirl-wind Saturday that included the now usual pre-move home improvement projects along with an oil change and complete cleaning for my 1994 Camaro, it was ready to roll. While only a V-6, the five-speed transmission really makes this a great long-distance road car. Cam and I had it packed (including my golf clubs for those lonely weekends!) and ready to go for a mid-morning departure on Sunday.

Sunday, May 13th - Day 1

Our goodbyes were a mixture of excitement and foreboding. I think Cameron was really jazzed and looking forward to the trip as a big adventure. I'm sure it didn't hurt either that he was getting a week's vacation from school. In fairness though, he had already felt the first effects of friends pulling away, once it became known that we were planning to move, and he was trying to adjust his sights toward our upcoming new future on the east coast. I, on the other hand, felt a small twinge of the feelings that our ultimate moving day departure would likely bring. All the emotion of saying goodbye to friends and our little piece of heaven flashed through my mind like a bad light show from a 1960s rock concert. I couldn't help feeling like such a failure to my family. I spent the better part of the first hundred miles or so playing the dreaded coulda, woulda, shoulda tape over and over and over again in my mind. It wasn't until we stopped that afternoon to grab a burger that I was able to leave that particular mental funk behind and begin to enjoy the company of one of my wonderful children, the freedom of the road and our ride east.

Cameron is a great car companion. He assumed the role of navigator and diligently followed and projected our progress on the road atlas we had included in our pre-departure packing. He had arranged with one of his teachers to receive credit for his time away from school if he kept a journal and provided a final trip report. This helped pass the time as well as focus his mind on something other than our move. While we talked about it freely, it wasn't a constant topic, and I don't think we spoke of it much after the first few hours. By dinner time we had reached Coeur d'Alene, Idaho, and after a quick stop for fuel (both the human and mechanical varieties), we pushed on into the developing darkness for another four hours of 75-80 mph cruising to reach Butte, Montana, and our first night's rest.

First day mileage: 650

Monday, May 14th - Day 2

The next morning I rolled out of bed at around 5:30 a.m., grabbed a quick shower and loaded our overnight gear back into the car. When I was ready to roll, I rousted Cam and got him upright just long enough for him to transition into the passenger seat without hardly missing a wink. We were two hours down the road before he woke up and joined me for the day. It wasn't long after that when we reached our first navigation hurdle of the trip and took the I-90 route as it turns south and separates from I-94 after Billings, Montana. Shortly thereafter, we came upon one of the mandatory historical stops on our trip: the Little Big Horn Battlefield National Monument, site of General George Custer's famous battle with Sitting Bull and the Sioux. We spent about an hour exploring the exhibits and walking the trails. I enjoyed the memory I had from my childhood doing the same things with my parents. Seeing this same ground again, although this time from the eyes of a parent watching my own child experience a real, living breathing piece of our nation's history, was very fun!!

Back on the road again, I-90 crosses into Wyoming and turns east again. We immediately noted the red color of the asphalt and increased construction activity. I chuckle at this memory, as Cameron can really ramble on and inquire about a subject when he is truly interested. By late afternoon we achieved our second historical objective of the day: Mount Rushmore, South Dakota, just outside of Rapid City. Again, I recalled a family trip from my youth, although my fading memory did not come close to the reality of actually seeing this magnificent monument in person again. I think Cam was truly awestruck; I know I was. The setting of the Black Hills is beautiful, and the contrast with this larger-than-life artwork carved out of the side of a mountain is absolutely breathtaking. If you haven't been yet, go! You won't regret it. As it turned out, this was to be my first of three visits in 2001.

After a brief stop in the great gift shop, we headed back to the car and made our way to the Interstate for a few more hours on the road before calling it a day. At some point after dark, we made a gas stop and upon returning to the highway, found that our headlights no longer worked on the standard low-beam setting. With no choice but to continue to the next major town of Mitchell and seek repairs in the morning, I tried my best to avoid tailing long-haul truckers too closely with high beams only. I was really tired by the time we found a place to stop in Mitchell at around 11:00 p.m.

Second day mileage: 871   Total mileage: 1468

Tuesday, May 15th - Day 3

The next morning we located the nearest Chevy dealer and had their Service department diagnose and fix the light problem. When we hit the road again, it was nearly lunch time, and we needed to make a choice about our route for the rest of the trip. Just outside of Sioux Falls, South Dakota, I-90 intersects with I-29 running north-south. If we were going to avoid the metropolitan Chicago area, we should take I-29 and drop south to hook up with I-80 east for a straighter shot into New Jersey. My main concern was arriving in time for work on Friday so that Cam could come to the city and spend the day at work with me. I also had a surprise for him on Friday after work. The company softball team (of which I was the oldest member at age 45) was playing a game in Central Park and I thought that would be a great experience; I didn't want to miss it. But by day three, I was pretty confident of our progress, so I told Cam that I thought we had time to take in a few sights in Chicago, where I had worked much earlier in my career. We landed in downtown Chicago at the Drake Hotel (a Chicago landmark) at around 8 p.m. After checking in and grabbing a quick shower, we called home to give our daily progress report and then headed out to find a good steak to balance out all of the fast food we had been eating lately. We walked around a bit afterwards and then hit the sack.

Third day mileage: 640   Total mileage: 2108

Wednesday, May 16th - Day 4

Before leaving Chicago, Cam and I grabbed a cab and headed down to the Loop and the Chicago Board of Trade building. I wanted him to see the trading floor and put some reality into the understanding he was developing about trading and financial markets. We looked up an old friend whom I had lost contact with and he generously took the time to get us a floor pass and personal tour of the trading arena. I saw several other old pro's I had known in younger days, and they took Cameron under their collective wing for twenty minutes or so and gave him a great tour. At one point they had him right at the edge of one of the agricultural pits when the opening bell rang and all hell broke loose. Needless to say, this was eye opening to him, and he still talks about it today. Next, we moved on to the Sears Tower and took the express elevator up to the top level observation deck. Wow, what a view! It was now nearly noon and we needed to check out of the Drake and resume our trip east, so we headed back to do just that.

Later that day, we found ourselves in Ohio, just before Cleveland, where I-80 splits off southward from I-90 and its northern route around the shore of Lake Erie. We took the I-80 route and rolled on into Pennsylvania, reaching the town of Washington before we called it a night.

Fourth day mileage: 483   Total mileage : 2591

Thursday, May 17th - Day 5

With only another 350-400 miles to go today, I let us sleep in until 9:00 a.m. After a food and fuel stop, we hit the road again for our last day and final destination: Bayonne, New Jersey, and my tiny attic apartment. I will never forget the excitement we both felt, but Cameron's was more visible when we cleared the foothills of New Jersey as I-80 heads toward New York City, and there they were: the Twin Towers. These beacons in the skyline seemingly shouted out to us "you made it, here's New York, the Big Apple!!" I can close my eyes even today and see the look on my son's face as he caught his first glimpse of a new world, his new world, three thousand miles from the shores of Puget Sound and all things familiar. Yet his youthful excitement and smile provided me with all the strength I needed. This was going to work. "It won't be easy, but we can all do this," I thought to myself. We rolled in to

Bayonne at about 6 p.m., grabbed some dinner and hit the sack early. I think we were both pretty tired, and I didn't have a problem admitting I was looking forward to a day off from behind the wheel.

Fifth day mileage: 373   Total mileage : 2964

Day In the City

Friday morning brought a significant change to our recent routine—we walked!! Three blocks down and one block over from my apartment was the end-of-the line station for the light rail train that ran from Bayonne through Jersey City. It was very new, well maintained, reasonably priced and overall very convenient. With only a handful of thirty-second stops between Bayonne and our exit station one block from the edge of the Hudson River in Jersey City, the ride didn't take 15 minutes. From there, we opted to stay above ground for the view rather than take the PATH subway into the city, and so we hopped aboard the water taxi for the ten-minute ride across the Hudson to Manhattan. The dock on the New York side is right at the foot of the World Financial Center complex, which has a wonderful waterside promenade that is always alive with people. Restaurants, a marina, shops and a theater are just some of the things found there. Entering the nearest building leads to a skywalk pedestrian bridge over West Street and right into the lobby of 1 World Trade Center, the

North Tower and home to my employer, TradeWeb, on the 51st floor.

I can't say anything particularly exciting happened at the office that day. Cameron met most everyone and spent a fair amount of time just enjoying the scenery. The view of the harbor and lower Manhattan was spectacular, with the Statue of Liberty in plain sight. We ate breakfast at the Port Authority cafeteria and ventured downstairs to the Trade Center mall for lunch. Before long it was approaching 5:00 p.m., and the softball team began changing into our play clothes and jerseys (I still have mine) and gathering all the gear. We headed downstairs to the subway for the trip uptown to Central Park and the ball field where we were scheduled to play.

The subway is very foreign to most West Coasters and perhaps in particular to those hailing from Bainbridge Island. At rush hour it is absolutely crazy; trying to stay together with a group of eight or ten people is a real challenge. We had to change trains once or twice, and at one point I thought I had lost Cam, but he had been taken under the wing of one of my teammates, who was a native New Yorker and Cam was receiving a full blown, yet expedited lecture on New York life and subway riding in particular. The game was fun, but I think Cam would have enjoyed himself more had he been allowed to play. Nonetheless, Central Park, baseball, warm weather and friends made for a great evening, topped off with dinner at a local pub and the ride home through the city. All in all, Cameron came away with a true New York experience.

End of the Road

Saturday was spent exploring various communities in and around Freehold, New Jersey. One of my co-workers at the time, and someone I have come to call a good friend, invited Cam and I to his home and treated us like family. Our guided tour included much of the local community of Red Bank, the Jersey shore with their great parks and even the "star" locator home tour of New Jersey locals like Springstein and Bon Jovi. Pretty cool!! I know that much of the effort on my friends part was an attempt to show both Cam and myself that lots of families just like us live here and have fun and a normal life. I don't know how successful he was, but it seemed like a worth-while exercise and I will always be grateful for his concern and interest in my family's upcoming move.

Regarding the trip overall, I can honestly say that this week was some of the very best Dad-Son time I have ever spent. It was so good, in fact, that I instituted a family tradition to be enjoyed by Cam's brother Alex and his sister Noelle when they turn twelve. We call it the 12-year-old road trip. As a matter of fact, Alex and I are scheduled for a trip to Arizona this spring (2005) to the Seattle Mariners spring training camp. I can't wait!

On Sunday, I had to say goodbye to my road warrior partner at the Newark International Airport, as I put him on a non-stop flight back home to Seattle. I think this was much more difficult for me, as Cameron seemed anxious to get home. I tried to keep a stiff upper lip until his face disappeared from the window as his plane taxied away from the gate. I felt depressed for the next several days, as the reality of our impending move seemed to take a giant leap forward in my mind. The intense week of solid one-on-one with Cameron reminded me how much we were all missing each other and how critical it was to permanently solve the problem by relocating to the east coast. It was the constant thought of achieving this goal and recreating the ability to be home with my family each night that got me through the days and nights I would be spending alone in Bayonne. A band called Match Box20 had a popular song and album at the time titled Mad Season that spoke of feeling stupid, and being lost and without hope, and how a person could find themselves in a state of ruin. It became a personal anthem of sorts post-Deposit Software and pre-9-11 that summer of 2001 in my tiny attic inferno apartment. Who could have known just how mad a season we were about to enter?

CHAPTER 3

Moving East

Schools, Bedrooms and Commute

Over the course of the next five or six weeks, I was successful in my efforts to finish exploring enough of New Jersey's neighborhoods and communities to feel good about leasing a house in Freehold. The school system had checked out wonderfully and my commute would be doable, albeit significantly extended from the one I was beginning to enjoy from Bayonne. The house, while significantly smaller than our home on Bainbridge Island, was something I thought we could squeeze into. It had an oversized, level, fenced back yard and was located in a neighborhood with a community pool and tennis and hoops courts. All in all, it wasn't bad. Of course, Arlene hadn't exactly had an actual look.

I had, however, taken several rolls of film and forwarded them home for her to review. She said she trusted me completely. I recall at this point that I had a flash recollection of the old line "Give them enough rope to hang themselves," but I quickly told myself that I had done the best I could and that it would work out just fine.

The schools in Freehold that the children would attend had been carefully scrutinized by Arlene and several of her friends. She liked what she saw in writing and, combined with what I could view in person, we both felt like this part of the move would be fine. Not to discount in any way the significance of the sacrifices made and the pain endured by Cam, Alex and Noelle, but Arlene and I both knew that if their school environment and neighborhood community were good, time would, as they say, heal all wounds.

Commuting would soon take on a whole new life, as Freehold was a good fifty-minute drive in the morning from the Park And Ride at Liberty State Park where I could catch the light rail and follow the rest of the route I had been using from Bayonne. I suspected that in the evening, the time required to make the trip home could potentially double. I have had long commutes before of an hour or more in freeway traffic, so I more or less understood what would be involved. Besides, this was a basic requirement of east coast living if you wanted an affordable, residential neighborhood atmosphere for your family. I did, and I would certainly do whatever it took to make it happen.

Neighbor Helping Neighbor

Back on Bainbridge, Arlene was going full tilt, organizing the effort to actually make the move happen. She was contacting schools at both ends, holding yard sales, and getting the moving company to survey, estimate and schedule our pickup and delivery. Once these dates were identified, I was able to arrange my travel back to Bainbridge one last time, and also schedule some vacation time off work. One of the most heart wrenching tasks was to find homes for our two dogs. Molly, our young Golden Retriever, had only been with us for six months or so, but Shadow, our Alaskan Malamute, had been a member of the family for over seven years. I still don't know how I could have done this to him, but our new quarters did not allow for a dog. I asked a former Deposit Software employee and good friend, who provides shelter to "rescued" dogs, for help, and he and his wife stepped up to the plate and said they would care for him. God, that was so hard for all of us. He is a very cool animal and extremely good with the kids. Noelle learned to walk holding his tail, and at the beach he would let the kids pour sand on him when they were little.

Arlene and I can't even begin to describe how our community of friends on Bainbridge Island and the greater Seattle area helped us keep our sanity through it all. We both can always catch a smile by reflecting back on the huge effort so many gave so selflessly. So many parties, so little time!! Throughout all of my prior time spent cross-country commuting, Arlene and her girlfriends would have a "support night," usually at our house and usually on the third Thursday of the month which came to be called the Cheetah Club. It was a women's-only book club of sorts that didn't read much, but really liked and needed a night out. It was a gift that kept on giving: good friends, good times and plenty of good memories.

It was August 8th when we finally reached the actual packing day for the move. The crew worked hard but soon realized that the number of hours estimated was woefully inadequate for the job at hand, so Arlene joined the crew. When we have moved in the past, Arlene would disappear and leave the premises during much of the pack and load, as it is just too upsetting for her. This time, however, she was stuck doing much of the wrapping and boxing for the better part of two days. Finally on the third day, when the van and loaders arrived, the packing crew was done and she found some "away" time. She took the kids, and they visited a few friends one last time. I stayed behind, but my presence at the house was not much more than a formality after I told the driver that everything gets loaded. It took the better part of the day for his crew of four to load the big van with all of our things. I didn't really believe it would all fit, but then I'm not a mover!

It is strange, I suppose, to reflect back on the last day, Friday, August 10th and not have a really clear memory, but I think that my mind has somewhat erased many of the day's details or perhaps simply erected a permanent barrier blocking them from recall out of an unconscious self-protection mechanism. I do recall watching in numbed silence as the van backed down our street and disappeared over a small hill before coming to a corner large enough for the driver to turn around. I know I pictured the next time I would see that rig would be in Freehold at the new house. Between now and then, I realized what lay ahead was a long trip, one much different from the one Cam and I had enjoyed earlier in the year. This one would begin like a wake and require much more effort to provide both Arlene and the kids with a positive outlook and help in dealing with the change. I wasn't sure if I had that in me, but knew I had to push my grief and sorrow aside in order to help them deal with theirs.

A short while later, we loaded everyone in the packed Suburban and headed out for our new life on the East coast. Just about everyone cried to some degree, and as we crossed the Agate Pass bridge on the north end of the Island, Arlene recalls me saying quietly to her, "I wonder if we'll ever be as happy as we were here . . . ." I recall that her stoic silence was deafening.

Another Road Trip

The boys had helped pack the car for this trip and, of course had included the road trip electronic package which included a small TV / VCR player, Playstation II, headphones, and a collection of videos, games and music CDs. At Arlene's suggestion, the kids decided to watch a video that would hopefully distract and entertain them for the first couple of hours.

The headphones were really great, as we didn't have to listen to the movie, and they couldn't hear us talk. Wait a minute, maybe that's why they wore the things so much!! Anyway, this gave me and Arlene a chance to talk semi-privately, although there was lots of silence as well. What could we say? The decision to do what we were now implementing had been made months before. We both knew this day would come, but of course the reality was more painful than the plan. Personally, I could no longer avoid the searing truth that my family was giving up everyone and everything familiar to them to pay for my failed business and my inability to gain employment in Seattle. This was more than I could bear, and by the time we stopped in Montana for the night, I was reacting in the worst possible way. I was angry and frustrated and, at one low point, stupidly yelled out that maybe everyone would be better off without me and that they should stay on Bainbridge and that I should live alone in New York. We all cried and as Arlene calmed us down, we held each other tight and told each other that we could make it if we stuck together, and that our emotions were a natural reaction to today's traumatic departure. I have since prayed many times for forgiveness for that night and for God's help to cleanse my family's memories of the image of their earthly provider completely frustrated and lost in his own pity and shame.

Early into the second day's drive, we found ourselves at the Little Big Horn with the opportunity to be tourists just like everybody else. This was a key turning point in the trip and was reinforced later that day at Mount Rushmore as well.

We had an adventure on our hands and by the end of the day there were more smiles and laughs to be seen and heard than had been the case for many days. We bypassed Chicago this trip as by day four, Arlene and I both recognized it was more important to get there and out of the confines of the car than to take in more tourist activities and prolong the trip. The greater number of travelers changed the trip dynamics by shortening the driving day with later starts and earlier finishes as well as more potty, food and rest stops than when it was just me and Cam. Regardless, the days passed by and our only difficulties were of the traditional variety when riding in the car for a long time with children. There was one thing, though that after the second day became a great source of fun and sometimes outright hilarity. The only pet we were able to retain and move with us was Chucky, our twenty-two pound, extra-large size, black-and-white, laid back cat. Each night at the motel, Arlene and I would attempt to get him from the car to the room. I don't think we did it the same way twice, as he was always ready to get out of the car and stretch his legs. By the third night, one of us came up with the brilliant idea to put him in a pillow case before getting out of the car for the ride up the elevator to the room. Needless to say, he wasn't thrilled and I was holding this howling, thrashing pillowcase as I tried to slide unnoticed into the elevator, where I have to shift my grip and he appears out the top. No problem: the door is closed but then we both realize that those little boxes in the corner of the elevator's ceiling are cameras and that all of our little stealth efforts are being viewed, and we just lose it. We laughed so hard the kids thought we had gone nuts. All in all, the three-thousand-mile trip went very well after that horrible first night, and everyone seemed to get excited as we got closer and closer to our destination. We pulled into Freehold and the new neighborhood on the sixth day: Wednesday, the 15th of August, 2001.

Honey, I Shrunk the House!

Upon receiving a call that evening from the moving van driver that he wouldn't be arriving until Friday, we found a reasonable motel with a pool near the New Jersey Turnpike and took two rooms. Nothing like living out of a suitcase after living out of your car for a week!! Even Chucky seemed to be fed up with the lack of steady accommodations and the accompanying inconveniences. We explored our new town over the next several days and I showed Arlene and the kids where the mall was, their new schools and the local market. Another phone call came on Friday morning from our driver, who was now going to be delayed until Saturday or possibly Sunday due to mechanical problems. AAHHHHH!!! So the kids played in the pool, and Arlene and I took turns napping and keeping watch.

Sunday morning after breakfast we loaded up the Suburban one last time, checked out of our rooms, and headed into Freehold and our new home to meet the moving van, which was finally going to arrive between ten and eleven that morning. We were all inside further exploring the house and mentally planning where we wanted certain things to go. Decisions were made like which bedroom the boys would share and which one would be Noelle's. I heard the air brakes on the big rig at about 10:30 a.m. when he pulled to a stop in front of the house. After a few quick hellos and shuffling of cars, the van backed smoothly into our little five-house-cul-de-sac, and the crew began unloading.

I suppose like anywhere in America, a moving van being unloaded will bring people out to meet the new neighbors and kids to see who might become a new playmate. Freehold was no exception. Our immediate neighbors were very friendly and generously offered to help in any way they could. I recall Arlene and I exchanging smiles when we watched the kids each be discovered by multiple children their own ages. Most of the day, however, was spent directing the constant stream of stuff being disgorged from the side door and down the ramp of the moving van. I took up the pole position and made the preliminary routing choice of in the house or to the garage. Arlene handled the room routing once something made it inside. By 3 p.m. we were barely halfway done, but the garage was nearly full and the house looked like a giant maze of boxes, picture packs and furniture that was both too large and too plentiful. Around 7 p.m. the movers loaded their gear and put the ramp away. As they pulled out, Arlene and I waved goodbye and were left standing alone in the most amazingly overcrowded dwelling I have ever been in. We just kept giving each other a look that said, "good grief, what a mess!" We didn't know whether to laugh or cry. Neither car was in the garage and had no prospect of ever getting there; the living room couldn't even be navigated; the kitchen was nearly walled off by stacks of boxes from the adjoining family room; and the boys' bedroom had about three square feet of space to stand between their beds. I think Noelle's room and the master bedroom were the only rooms even halfway standing up to the onslaught of Johnson family possessions.

We had gotten pizza and sodas for the crew and ourselves around 5 p.m. so we didn't need to go out for dinner. Everyone was exhausted, and we simply focused on finding enough covers for everyone. I think the boys gave up looking after a while and simply used sleeping bags that first night, as their bedding was missing in action amid the cardboard chaos. Tomorrow was Monday and I had to be back at work, so Arlene and I crawled into bed at around 11 p.m. and found sleep quickly in our new home, for the first time, in a place far, far away.

Seeking Normalcy

Well, here we are. We did it. Home every night and still some summer vacation left to boot! All things considered, the move appeared to have gone about as well as we could have hoped to expect. We were safe, together, and looking at least semi-ready to start our new life. My first full week of commuting found me happily trying different routes in order to maximize my home time. It was so great to simply be together again that I didn't give the drive a second thought. In fact, we often headed out soon after my arrival home to catch dinner, explore the mall, hit the movie theater or just do the grocery shopping. Like I said, I didn't mind this one bit as we were all together. When we stayed home, we walked after dinner, and the kids rode their bikes and played with new friends. The community pool was a favorite, and I think the short bike ride through the neighborhood gave them confidence regarding their new surroundings.

Of course there was lots of work to do. Arlene spent most of her days those first few weeks seeking to create some order out of the complete chaos within the house. We decided that first weekend that we needed to rent a storage unit so we could remove as much as we could to an off-site location. By Sunday evening the 26th, I had shuffled things sufficiently to get at least one car out of the driveway and into the garage. It seems silly now, but at the time this offered us a small victory in our battle for more organization in our living environment. Every little bit seemed to help, and the kids took to cheering every time another box was flattened and set on the curb for the recycling truck.

During my explorations for living quarters, I had discovered a really great golfing facility within ten minutes of our new home that incorporated a driving range, a nine-hole, par-three course, and a putt-putt style amusement course. I can't recall the first time we went, but it became a regular stop for us as both as a group and me with one of the kids. Cam had some lessons and Alex and Noelle loved to play the putt-putt course. I think Saturday mornings were a perfect time for these outings and a great way to get the weekends started with a little fun.

The start of school year was fast approaching, as the next weekend was Labor Day weekend. A welcome sense of normalcy was provided with the annual ritual of acquiring the requisite supplies and of course the new shoes and clothes for the next school year. One of our friends and her two great kids from Bainbridge Island had even paid us a visit, as she was attending a family wedding in nearby Princeton and needed a place to stay and stage, for the various weekend-long festivities. At the time, it was great to see a familiar face amid the chaos and I think it helped reconnect our two worlds for both Arlene and the kids, if even for only a few days.

The tour guide Cameron and I had from earlier in the year invited us to join his family and friends at their beach club over the Labor Day weekend, and we had a blast! I couldn't remember the last time I had participated in a serious, adult beach volleyball game, but my body would be reminding me most of the next week. Between muscles I forgot I had, and a full-blown sunburn, I felt a little worn out by Tuesday morning and was really looking forward to the week at work. On Wednesday, the 5th of September, I took Alex with me to Manhattan and a day at the office. It was the last day before school started, and Arlene and I both thought he could use the distraction. We had a great time riding the Path subway, water taxi and light rail just like his older brother had done months before in May. His eyes were like saucers when he saw how many big buildings there were in lower Manhattan. It was the Trade Center elevator rides, though, that really got his attention and I recall taking more than a few coffee breaks that day all the way down to the lobby and back.

With school's official start, Arlene had a bit more freedom of choice regarding her time, and she used it to make progress on the seemingly endless list of things to do. She had a couple of great neighbor Moms who helped with school info, sports activities, dancing classes, medical referrals and generally anything they could think of to make her job easier. I'm sure this included information about school-parent group meetings and activities. The first one in the new school year was going to be held on the following Tuesday, September 11th, and Arlene was scheduled to go. She was also scheduled to see a doctor about a worsening allergic reaction of some sort that was increasingly uncomfortable. At one point over the weekend of the 8th and 9th, we had to take her to the Emergency Care facility at a local hospital. I can't help but think that some of her condition was a result of stress. God knows she had plenty of that! There wasn't much she had tried that made her feel better over the last week or so. Unfortunately, the next week wouldn't offer much stress relief either. In fact, things were about to get significantly more stressful, something we wouldn't have believed possible at the time.

CHAPTER 4

The Exodus
September 11, 2001

I arrived at work that day a good half hour earlier than usual, even after my newly extended commute. It was a beautiful day, bright blue and sunny, but definitely early fall with a fairly crisp north wind of 15 or 20 knots. Not long after getting into the office, I realized I was missing something. I don't know how many of you have become friends with a pair of reading "cheater" half glasses and the requisite string device that hangs around your neck so you can keep track of them, but they seemed to have become indispensable to me ever sense the day I turned forty. Anyway, I discovered that I didn't have them with me that morning so I went back downstairs. The Trade Center had a sizable shopping mall under and between the Twin Towers. There was a drug store down there, and I knew I could pop down and pick up another pair. I did that, and in the process of going back up, as I was waiting for the elevator, my boss and some of the other gentlemen from my firm exited from one of the cars. We waved hello and exchanged good mornings.

Once back upstairs in the office, I was standing with a couple of my team members chatting about a presentation we were preparing for later in the week when all of sudden—BOOM!! There's this really loud explosion, and a huge shaking and swaying of the building that literally lifted me off the floor and caused me to fall into a nearby wall. Over the next ten to fifteen seconds we were all trying to right ourselves, and you could feel the building do one of those cartoon type boooiiinnggg, sending shudders that go right through the steel columns, concrete floor and into the soles of your feet. Being from the Northwest my first initial reaction was "Wow, that was a big quake!!" but then I have the reality sink in that I'm not in Seattle anymore, this is New York and they don't have many earthquakes. As I stand up, I see those around me doing the same and we are all beginning to look out over the tops of our cubicles. The north side of the building is about fifteen to twenty feet away, and you can see through the narrow, vertical windows that there is some type of debris raining down outside. I think I shouted "Get away from the windows" and then, at this point, a few of us looked at each other and almost simultaneously yelled that we needed to get out of here. We turned around away from the windows and headed south, out the office back door. Once in the hall, there was a stairwell entrance immediately to our left. Our little group from our side of the building slammed into the crash bar, which is the metal handle that opens the door into the stairwell, and took off running. We were able to run down seven or eight floors without seeing another person, without experiencing anything but our own breathing and the necessity of thinking about not falling, because we're running down concrete and steel stairs in street shoes. I know I had the sense of telling myself to slow down because breaking your leg at this point would not be a good idea. It wasn't a problem for long, because we soon did slowdown. We not only slowed down, we stopped. We ran into the back end of the line of all the other smart people from all the floors below us who had the same idea; get in the stairwell and get down.

We probably did not move, literally, another step at that point for a good fifteen minutes. With each passing minute you began to sense in your own body the amount of energy you were expending trying to tell yourself to stay calm. This is one of the first realities for me in witnessing the goodness that happened that day inside the stairwell. People helped each other. Whether they were physically more challenged at navigating the situation, or from an emotional standpoint simply needed reassurance, somebody reached out a hand, and gave that to them. Complete strangers. Whether it was just giving someone a hug, or giving someone an arm to lean on, or in my case I wound up holding a women's hand for the better part of the entire way down. I didn't know her at all, but that was what she needed. It was the extension of kindness as the natural reaction of people to this situation that stands out so starkly in my mind. In an environment of physical confinement, overcrowding and palpable anxiety and fear, the best in all of us presented itself. This was something very, very special.

As the line began to move again, the presence of fear was still with us. And while it was lit, warm and dry, you still had this impending sense of something's really not right. Every now and then you would overhear a conversation in fairly hushed tones of somebody who had been there when the buildings had been bombed in 1993. "Hey, don't panic, we just gotta walk down here, you'll be OK." As we continued down, the next real event was the second plane hitting the South Tower. As separated as those buildings were, the concussion and shock wave of the impact rattled through our little space as well, and you could actually see people's fear rise to a new level. It was another unknown: a very loud and disturbing movement of this huge building that you knew shouldn't be occurring in something this large.

I loved those buildings. I used take my lunch and go sit down on the Plaza level and put my back up against those channels of narrow windows and look up the more than one hundred stories above me and it would remind me of some of the great trees we have in the Pacific Northwest, really big, old growth timber. It was kind of like a piece of home, but I knew instinctively that something that big, made out of steel and concrete, should not be moving that way.

At some point the air quality began to deteriorate. It wasn't smoke, it was more of a kind of noxious odor, and what it turned out to be, which I didn't figure out until much later, was jet fuel. Any of the jet fuel from those planes that didn't burn off from the initial impact explosions and fireball was a liquid. Ultimately gravity was going to take over and the fuel would find any nook and cranny it could to head down. So after enough time, the odor began to permeate into the stairwell and you could notice the difference. Some people had more problems with that than others. People with asthma or breathing problems were starting to take off an article of clothing and covering their nose and mouth. Some people were smart enough to have a bottle of water, and they would wet down their makeshift masks and cover there mouth and nose to provide themselves some relief. Personally, I have a really bad habit of smoking one or two cigars every day, so I didn't really notice this as much as maybe somebody else did. But at some point, and I think we were in the upper mid thirty's 36, 37, 38 possibly, and somebody on a landing below me opens the door from the stairwell to that floor. The strangest thing then occurred, just like the magical sense of what we would all remember as the "pied piper". The cool air that came off of that floor into the stairwell was like a magnate. The last person on that landing going down, in front of the person who opened the door, continued to go down with the line of people, while the other people on that landing and everybody on the stairs immediately above them started to walk out of that door, fill up the foyer and just start milling around. When I got out the door, as I followed the flow of people out too, there were already 50 or 60 people there. As I moved about ten or fifteen feet away from the door, I had a physical reaction. My legs locked up, and the person behind me bumped into me and the people behind them bumped into them like dominoes and started to fall over. I stepped out of line to gain my balance and looked at the people from my group and said, "We have to get out of here." This is one of those points I can't explain, because I was just compelled to do this, so we pushed our way back into the stream of people still coming out the door and made our way back into the stairwell, where we were able to resume the march down and join up with the line of people who had continued in front of us. I don't have any evidence to support this, but it is my belief that not everybody who chose to stop on that floor that day made it out of the building. If you stayed too long, there was a point where you weren't going to get out. I believe very much that was God's hand in my life for helping me be able to do that.

As we continued down, we were moving at a fairly consistent pace, but you were also inwardly still trying to focus on maintaining your own stability for lack of a better term. At some point I know I thought I was hearing things. I thought I heard laughter, and if there was one thing you probably wouldn't expect to hear in there, was a lot of laughter, like somebody telling a joke or something. But I thought I did, and it kind of wafted in and out a little bit, and then some clapping came with it but still just fading in and out. Until the point where it was consistent enough that I knew it was real, that my mind wasn't playing tricks on me, yet I still didn't know what it was. I tried to look down the narrow railing which is only 2 –3 inches wide to see if I could see anything below, but of course I can't, there is no peripheral vision from that point of view. But I know there was something going on, and as I got down another flight, it just kept getting louder, and as I turned a corner and started down from another landing, I can see the people on the landing below are actually clapping and I'm thinking "What?? What??" And then you see him. It's a New York City Firefighter. He's turning the corner on that landing below, and he's marching up the stairs in your row with a reel of hose on one shoulder, and his steel pry-bar in the other hand, with his air tanks and his mask and he's just marching up those stairs, one at a time, telling you that it's going to be OK, your going to get out, keep calm. And after you saw the first one, they just kept coming. There was Port Authority policemen, NYPD policemen, Plainclothes detectives, and of course the Firemen. I didn't have the sense of this until afterwards when we were outside, but imagine, and this is another perspective that I need to make sure I mention, while you readers I presume are all seeing this on TV, we're in a concrete vertical tunnel. We don't have a clue what's going on. All of you had a much better idea about what's happening, we know nothing and thank God these guys aren't saying anything. They rolled up to those buildings, got out, looked up into the sky, saw what you were seeing on TV, and yet came in to do their job. Where do we get men and women like that to do this kind of job? It doesn't matter if it's in a big city environment or a small town, like Bainbridge Island. The self sacrifice and the mentality of the people that choose to do this job, boggles my mind. That is one of the hugely positive things that I've come to take away from my experience. We have all seen those red lights, or heard that siren and half the time our reaction is "oh man, I'm going to fast", or worse, in some places people don't even pull over. Well those guys are going to help somebody, get out of their way!! It's just a great feeling, knowing more about that kind of community, that I'm extremely proud to have experienced and want to pass on to you.

Well, as we continue on our path down, things do open up a bit and we're able to move a little bit faster. Somebody actually starts to sing the old "99 Bottles of Beer on the Wall" song, when we're down in the low to mid teens. You can smell we're going to get out of here. However, there's one little trick waiting for us at the bottom. For some reason the design of the building had the stairwells go a flight below the lobby level and then come back up. The sprinkler system has been on for about an hour now, as that is about how much time has transpired, and for some reason either the drain was plugged, or there was no drain, as the designers may have forgotten that requirement. As we approach the bottom, there is a fireman on our side and another on the stairs going back up and they shove you across this little lake. Now you're completely drenched down to your underwear and stepping out into the lobby. This is not something I dwell on a lot; suffice it to say it was not a pretty place. You were trying to focus on doing what people were telling you to do and did not have a lot of extra time to look around. They didn't want us to go to the immediate outside exit as this was on West Street, and they were bringing all the rescue equipment down the West Side Highway. I later learned that the real reason was the risk of being killed by falling debris or people jumping from the inferno above. They told us to go interior to the building. Back by the drug store that I had bought my glasses at earlier that morning, telling us "hurry but don't run". If there's something that is a complete oxymoron is wearing leather loafers on a wet marble floor with a hurry but don't run instruction. Your body wanted to go faster than you were able to stay upright. We worked our way around the shopping area until we came to the other side of the complex, and hiked up an escalator that had a mini waterfall rushing down it, and we stepped out into that bright sunshine and clear blue sky. It was only after stepping about fifteen feet away from the building overhang that I could actually now turn around and look up and see what the rest of the world had been watching on TV for the last hour or so. I am here to tell you that it was the most surreal, unbelievable sight that my eyes will ever see. It was right out of a movie. You could not believe nor ever forget what you were seeing at that point: the mountains of smoke and debris pouring forth from those buildings; the thousands of people milling about, looking lost and in shock; the poor souls whose only choice was to leap to their death or be consumed by the flames. All of this imagery flooded into my brain and weighed heavily on my heart. It was simply too much to process all at once and my attention turned back toward my coworkers.

Our little group, there were six or seven of us together from our firm, went across Church Street. People started to think about a cell phone or wallet, none of which I had, as I had left all my things upstairs. I stepped away from the group and went over behind a parked car where I got down on my knees and thanked God for getting me out of that building. His answer I got back was "You need to call your wife."

I feel very, strongly about the fact that my wife and my family have carried the burden of this experience, because the whole time when your involved in something like this, you know you're ok, you're still breathing, I was still walking, I know I'm out, but she didn't have that luxury, and neither did Cameron who was at his new school. In the process from splitting up from the group, I knew that if I could get across the Hudson River, I could, if I had to, walk the 35 or 40 miles home to Freehold. I didn't know how long it would take, but it would be physically possible. If I went the other way, south and east, where the Police and other First Responders were trying to get everyone to go, I knew I would have a really difficult time getting back to New Jersey. So I said goodbye and broke away from the group and headed north up Broadway. I was about 5 or 6 blocks away when the South Tower, the second to get hit but first to fall, began to come down. I'll tell you that the second most amazing thing that my eyes have ever seen is turning around at the initial horrific sound of that and seeing thousands of people running up the street in your direction. I turned around and took off running. I was fortunate in that I had headed upwind and from where I was the dust cloud didn't get that far uptown. From here, I just randomly tried to make my way north and west. The police had streets blocked off and as they got into an argument with someone, I would take that opportunity to run down the street that they were arguing with that person about, in order to get myself where I thought I wanted to go. By now, I'm running randomly down streets in lower Manhattan and I go by a window, and look in, and there is my boss, who I had seen leaving the building when I was waiting for the elevator. Now what are the odds of that, in downtown Manhattan, running into them on this or any other day? I go inside and recognize the place. It's another Wall Street technology company that I had visited a year or two ago while marketing for Deposit Software. They still have their bandwidth up and going, and had been able to access our computers in order to get the names and phone numbers of people at home. They immediately quizzed me about who I'd seen out of the building, who I was with and where I had last seen them. We were able to make a telephone connection to my boss's parents in Kennebunkport, Maine, and gave them this information, and they were able to make long distance phone calls back into New York and New Jersey from out of state. During this time, our building, the North Tower also collapsed. We watched it live on CNN while hearing and feeling the actual collapse just a few blocks away. Our helpers in Maine were able to get reach Arlene and that's how she found out I was out of the building and was okay. Unfortunately, however, the call came a little late, as she had just finished watching my building collapse live on TV.

PHOTO ALBUM

Oil painting by Arlene.

Cameron and Earl at the
beginning of our road
trip to NY/NJ.

Cameron at the Little
Big Horn Battlefield
in Montana.

Cameron at Devil's Tower
in Wyoming.

View from the water taxi crossing the Hudson River from NJ to Manhattan.

Cameron in NY at the World Financial Center Plaza 1 block West of WTC.

The whole
family at
the Little
Big Horn.

Alex, Noelle & Cameron at Mount Rushmore.

Alex at the World
Financial Center
Plaza, 1 block
West of WTC.

Alex at the light
rail station in
Jersey City.

Kids' first day
of school in
Freehold NJ,
September, 2001.

Earl and Arlene at the NJ Shore, Labor Day weekend, 2001.

The house in Freehold, NJ.

My fuzzy friends, Shadow (L) and Sabrina (R).

Darryl on stage.

Darryl Worley & Earl at concert 3/16/05.

CHAPTER 5

Stairwell to Heaven

One Path, Two Destinations

This chapter's title was given significant thought and reflection prior to being assigned. I suppose these three words can have several meanings or interpretations, but for me, their simple message conveys the inescapable reality that for both our fallen Heroes and lucky survivors, those steel and concrete steps delivered each of them from evil. Some will be remembered by a numb nation. Many more will remain, seeking to understand their survival and the effect this fact will have on the rest of their lives. This book is a direct result of this process operating in my life.

It was not until after the first anniversary of 9-11 that I first began to recognize a pattern in my thoughts about surviving. I was always comparing my reality of a specific situation, like watching my kids in one activity or another, with that of Heroes less fortunate than myself. As a side note, I hope using the word hero to refer to anyone lost that day doesn't offend anyone. It is a reference I prefer, to better honor the totality of those lost, as opposed to a singular, more segregated labels like victims, office workers or First Responders. Not that each and every one of these groups doesn't or shouldn't have their own subset of recognized Heroes. I am simply trying to convey my belief that the whole is greater than the sum of the parts. That's all.

I eventually caught myself doing this mental comparison in a broadening circle of everyday activities: washing the car, reading a book, laughing at the dinner table and yes, even disciplining the kids. That last one always hits me hard because I worry about the children missing a Mom or Dad, Grandpa or Grandma or worst of all, possibly both. Who will provide them with the strength and leadership, with the example and belief in themselves? All those daily things that help to keep kids focused on success, while navigating down the twists and turns on life's path. My prayer is that their lives somehow, eventually gain a peace from the certain hell provided them on 9-11. My reflections on these now-recognized and welcome thoughts of comparison have resulted in a personal place of comfort for me. That is to say, the very fact that I do compare my life at a given point to one who is no longer here, has become my personal guarantee that as long as I have breath in my lungs and thought in my brain, they will not be forgotten.

Faces I've Seen

There is a part of my public speaking presentation about the process of exiting the North Tower via the northeast stairwell, when we meet up with the first person from the ground below, a New York City firefighter. And then another, and another, and another. Soon there are many: Firemen, NYC Policemen, Port Authority of NY/NJ detectives and other security personnel. Each has a face, each has a life and story to match. I am so happy so see them!! We all are! With the benefit of time passing, I am now able three years later to clearly and fully know why. Their very appearance at that time represented a huge reality for us. They came from below, at ground level, which we were so desperate to reach. This fact was no doubt subconscious to us at the time, as we cheered and clapped and breathed no small sigh of relief. If they can get up here, we all must have been thinking, we can get down there!

The true significance of this two-way traffic is at the heart of my perception now that ours was a world existing solely on a stairwell to heaven. We didn't, and couldn't know at the time, that the sea level heaven we were seeking would not be the same one attained by the brave souls climbing to secure our safe exit. It is this remembrance that shows me their faces. Not in any negative or haunting way, but rather in a profound sense of awe and amazement at the shear bravery and heroism I witnessed first hand that morning in September. These professionals saw live, in person, what most Americans, the whole world for that matter, were seeing only on TV. Those of us in the stairwell saw or knew nothing of this view until much later, when we had reached ground level and stepped outside. The fact that these Heroes drove up, got out, looked up, and then came in and continued up is in itself the single bravest act I will ever know. This realization is one of the most galvanizing thoughts I have. It is the fact that I was a direct beneficiary of the acts of these Heroes that drives me to speak out and share my witness with people. It is this fact that caused me to run for, and subsequently win, elected office as a Fire Commissioner, District #2, Kitsap County, for the Bainbridge Island Fire Department. And it is this fact of insurmountable bravery witnessed first hand, that empowers my desire to support, contribute and simply be part of, in some small way, this community of Heroes.

Each time I speak at a firehouse or in front of a group of First Responders, I pause on the faces I am seeing in the audience and can't help but think they are the same as the ones I saw in the stairwell. In many ways they are. Not the actual people of course, but what they represent: Heroes all, plain and simple. It is a powerful reflection and never fails to send shivers racing up and down my spine.

CHAPTER 6

Meanwhile, Back at the Ranch
(Written by Arlene R. Johnson)

The three kids and I get up like any other school day. Their Dad has already left and we have hardly heard him go. The new house is about half the size of our old house on Bainbridge Island, with the boys now sharing a bedroom and all three kids sharing one bathroom. There are still moving boxes everywhere and mounting evidence that we will never get everything to fit in this house comfortably. The kids seem to be sticking together and making the best of things, as they now only have each other. Every day is a new experience with new friends, neighbors, teachers, schools and even new cultures. Earl and I are amazed at how well they are adjusting to everything, but I guess compared to our crazy, mixed-up life before, this is in some ways better. There has been so much emotion in the last few months that I think we are all just sort of numb and worn out at the same time. Everyone is quieter than usual and struggling not to complain about everything being different. It is sad, yet I think we are trying to be optimistic that this new life could be even better than the old, once we get used to everything. We are definitely all trying to be brave and attempting to keep a stiff upper lip at all times.

The houses in this neighborhood are all very close together, and there are dozens of children from cultures all over the world including the Bronx! Cameron, Alex and Noelle are so tan this summer, as we have been spending much of our free time leading up to the start of school at the local community pool. We had no idea how hot the summers were here. All three of my children ride the same bus to their respective schools. This is a real blessing which seems to provide one more way for them to stick together. Off they go this morning. I pray that it isn't too weird for them and that they find a way to adjust to everything. The life we left was pretty perfect; the kids knew everybody and were comfortable in their surroundings. I worry that this is such a huge adjustment.

Just as a little side note, as I am writing this alone in my house, I have to get up to vomit in the bathroom. This reaction has come from out of nowhere; I was not even crying yet, like I normally do when I remember that day. I guess this physical reaction is brought on when I try to remember what 9-11 was like for me, from my perspective. I keep hoping that my reactions and feelings will dull in time, but that has not happened yet in over three years. I will forge ahead anyway.

After the children's bus leaves, I head back into the house to finish getting ready to go to my very first PTA meeting at the elementary school where Alex and Noelle are attending. Noelle is in first grade and is six, while Alex is in fourth grade and is 9 years old. Cameron, who is just about to turn twelve in nine days, is attending the junior high and is in sixth grade. By far and away this experience has been most difficult for Cameron. In the months leading up to our departure from Bainbridge, just about every friend he had decided not to be bothered with him because he was moving. I drove him to school the last two months back home just to avoid the school bus. I am going to this PTA meeting today, hoping to get a handle on what the school is like and how best to get involved to ease the adjustment.

I try to hurry, as I am afraid that I will get lost even though the school is not far. I have no sense of direction and can get lost fairly easily. I grew up outside of Los Angeles and got used to navigating the freeways; then we moved to the country, where I learned the country roads. Freehold is more like the San Fernando Valley I grew up in and getting lost scares me. It also apparently is against the law to use your cell phone when driving, but then who would I call? Earl is at work in the big city, and the only people I know are a few of his co-workers and two neighbors, both of whom are at work by this time. I am feeling very alone, yet trying to be brave like my children. How can I expect them to do something that I can not do myself? Luckily, I find the school with only one wrong turn. Making U-turns here is very different so I lose about ten minutes. When I eventually get to the school and find a place to park, I have to then find the meeting room. It is a large, sprawling school and I get lost again, twice. I must have looked lost, because at some point a preschool class finds me wandering the hallways, takes pity on me, and actually escorts me all the way there. I am feeling like a fish out of water now as I arrive five minutes late and rush to sit down in the back, as the meeting has already started, and I have not had time to meet anyone. If anything, I think my late arrival has annoyed the President, who was already talking. I sit down feeling uncomfortable in the sundress I chose to wear due to the heat, while everyone else is in business suits and pumps.

This group is not as laid back as the PTA on the west coast. It is apparent very quickly that they take this very seriously. They are discussing the success of the cookbook they wrote and published last year and how they are going to do it again. I was impressed, as at my children's old school we talked about this very same idea but never got it together. I'm taking notes and trying to catch up when somebody bursts into the auditorium and says that the World Trade Center has been bombed. Somebody asks which one? While I have never seen the buildings in person, I think to myself that it does not matter, as they are so close together either one could be damaged. My only real experience with high-rise buildings was living and working in Los Angeles. I worked on the 52nd floor of the First Interstate Bank building in downtown. It was the tallest building at the time in Los Angeles, with 72 floors.

I have also lived through three pretty major earthquakes while growing up in California. In Los Angeles, we had frequent earthquake and fire drills where we had to walk down the fifty-two flights of stairs. It was a good workout, but most unpleasant for a girl with claustrophobia. This is the first time it flashes through my mind that it will take Earl a long time to walk down the fifty something flights of stairs he has. I also started to question which floor he worked on, but I do know that he is in the tower with the large radio antennae on top. I get up from my seat in a fog, while thinking I should go home and wait to hear from him. He is the only one who will call me as I don't know anyone else in town.

Another woman got up, too, as I head out to leave, and while I think they went on with the meeting, I am not really sure. I am trying to remember where the front of the school is and hopefully my car. The other woman approaches and asks me my name. It turns out she is the sister of one of the two neighbors I know, and she had been sent to find me. She explained that their father works for AT&T on the eleventh floor of the same building as Earl's and she wanted to get home too. She reminded me that there will probably be no phone service, because most of the city's communications links were located on the top of the building. We stopped by the school office to make sure they were going to keep the kids unaware and to find out whether or not we should just leave them there. It dawns on me that I should not bring the kids home because Earl is a manager of a new product group and if some people were missing, some potentially scary communications could be going on at our house. I, like any mother, always want to protect and shelter my kids from anything unpleasant. Their safety and well being is number one to me at almost a compulsive level. I was already guilt ridden over what we had put them through up to this point.

I decide to leave the kids at school. I am sure this is best until I know exactly how bad it is and what is going to happen next. What if this is the last, semi-normal day of their life? I have to try to prepare myself for what is ahead and pull myself together. Did I feel I have it in me? NOOOO!!! I was already running on empty. I prayed to God to give me strength. The kind neighbors' sister walked me to my car and asked me if I can find my way home. I told her I hoped so. I knew she wanted to get to her own home so I resisted asking her to follow me. I am feeling utterly alone at this point, and it crosses my mind that this could be permanent. I cannot even go there. If I let my imagination take me there, I will be in a state of shock, paralyzed, immovable, and useless to everyone. I am shaking now, trying to hold back my tears so I can find my way home. I get in the car and pray I can make it home in one piece. Getting lost right now is not an option. Somehow I make it even after I take a few wrong turns, but I have made it back. I pull into the garage and shut the door quickly. I don't want to make contact with any of the neighbors right now. I don't want to have to remind them that yes, my husband works in one of the bombed buildings. Having strangers see me fall apart and feel sorry for me is not something I can handle right now. I must find out where Earl is, nothing else matters.

As I sit in the car trying to collect myself, it crosses my mind for the first time that Earl is a big, strong, healthy man whose family is his first priority. He will move heaven and earth to get out of that building, but, and it is a big but, he is also kind and compassionate and if someone needed his help he would be there at his own risk. So the quality I love most about my husband could be his downfall. He could easily die a hero. In fact I am positive that he is helping others right now. He is a leader, and if required, he is going to help as many people as he can. These thoughts give me some temporary comfort. I am so proud of the man I share my life with, but I am also afraid that our life together may be over. I am dreading the hours ahead, knowing that my life and my young family's life might be about to change forever. I question myself if I am strong enough to deal with my new future. I dread waiting and I dread finding out. What if it is the worst? The feeling is surreal, with time standing still in an awful place.

With little thought, I finally jump out of the car and race into the house to check the phone. It was dead, just like my cell phone. I race upstairs to the computer, but no internet connection either, no ability to send or receive email. It almost feels like a power outage. I run back downstairs to the phone in the kitchen, remembering there is a separate stand-alone answering machine; maybe it is still working. It blinks a red number ten, meaning ten messages, and my mind flashes, "Oh God this can't be good." One of my oldest friends back in Seattle was first on the tape. She is a good Catholic girl; her voice is like death warmed over. "R (my nickname), it is not good, it does not look good. Oh my God. How will he get out?? I am here or there, whatever you need. It is not good." Her voice is a terrified whisper. She has put into words all my scary thoughts like only a true friend can do. I must try to comfort her, to reassure her but I cannot because everything she is saying is true. It is not good. I know I can count on her now in the crisis, but what will I do for the rest of my life? What kind of life would I have without Earl? I cannot bear to think about it. How will my children survive without their father? He is the best father ever, their lives would be destroyed, empty, they could never be happy again. "Please God, don't do this to them," I beg, "they are so innocent, and they love him so much they cannot survive this. It would destroy us all." I am feeling so helpless I can hardly stand or move. I know I have to listen to the rest of the messages yet somehow, I know none of them are from Earl. At around 9:20 a.m. it is too soon. He is still getting out of the building.

The rest of the messages are from other friends and family, all saying they will help, they will get in a car and drive out to get me and the kids. It should be comforting, but it is not. I cannot let myself think about trying to get my family back to the west coast without Earl. It is like a cliff I can't jump off. I know the rest of the scenario is disastrous, and I won't go there. It is too horrible. I feel if I think about life without him, I will shut down and die. I will just stop breathing, stop moving, and die in a heap right there in Freehold, New Jersey. The thing that keeps me going is my hope and faith that somehow I will get my miracle, I will be one of the lucky ones, and I will get to keep my husband. Somehow I will get lucky, I will be blessed. "Why not?" I ask, "Why not me?" This thought coincides with a message from another close friend. She is a deeply religious person, and she is practically screaming on the answering machine tape, "He is not dead, he is not dead!" I want to believe her so much, when she says that she would know if he was dead, and he is not. He is all right, he is okay, and I am not to give up hope. Her strong words empower me, as I try to follow her admonition to stay strong in my faith. I am to keep believing that he is coming home to me. Everything will be okay, it will all work out, and her whole family is there to support us. Her conviction is strong, and I chose to believe her words and cling to hope and faith.

The messages were finished, and the answering machine was silent, there was no more communication for me for now. Somehow I managed to get back upstairs to my bedroom, fall on my bed and turn on the TV. They were showing the planes crashing into the towers over and over again. "Oh my God, this is horrible, it wasn't a bomb, we are being attacked!" It suddenly dawned on me, "what if I am wrong about the floor he is on? What if it is not fifty-one?" I worked on the fifty-second floor of a building in Los Angeles; maybe I am mixed up. My brain is on overload, as I start tearing the room apart looking for one of Earl's business cards or piece of stationary showing the floor number. I can see on the TV that the plane has hit sort of high on the building with the large antenna; maybe he is below it. That would give me hope. "Why is this room so messy? Where is my phone book? Oh yeah, we just moved across the country a couple of weeks ago." My life is upside down in every aspect. I find my address book, it has his business card, and it is indeed the 51st floor. Relief floods my body for thirty seconds until I glance up at the TV. One of the towers comes crashing down. It implodes and all that is left is a giant smoking pile of funeral ash. I, like the rest of the world can not believe my eyes. It cannot be real. How can a building fall onto itself? It is impossible. This is America, we build buildings to withstand everything. There is no way!!!! I watched it over and over and over and still could not comprehend it. It is a horrible scenario that never even entered my mind, not in a million years. I am paralyzed, transfixed to the TV images, and time stands still. I feel empty, void of all emotion, and then after a little while the other tower collapses. Oh, my God. All hope is gone, lost forever. How could anyone survive this catastrophe? Nobody would be prepared for this turn of events. It is like nothing I could ever have imagined. It is as if the earth has fallen off its axis, and the world has come to an end. Now I don't want to answer the phone, ever. I don't want to know how he died. I just want it over. Everything. How can I go on living? I don't want to live in this new, crazy world where buildings fall down and there is no Earl. How can I go on? There is no way, and just as quickly as I have these over-powering thoughts, I remember my children.

I have no choice but to live; I cannot die with Earl. I have to go on and put a life back together without him. We have shared a life for 17 years; what other life is there?

Where should I live? We are in a city 3,000 miles from everyone and everything familiar, and my life is over. I have no plan, no future, nor do I really want one. I just know I have to help my kids. For the next two hours, I kneel on the floor in front of the TV, alone, praying, sobbing, and gasping for air. Chuckey is near me and he too is terrified. He has never seen or heard me like this. I am begging for a miracle, begging for my husband's life, too terrified to imagine a life without him.

I have a little experience with someone close losing her husband and leaving behind young children. I have planned a funeral, spoken at it, and rocked fatherless children to sleep. "Please don't let this happen to me," I beg. "I can't do it, I am not strong enough. Earl is too good. The world needs him, I need him. Please spare him. I will do anything."

Then the first call came, the phones are working again. It is Earl's boss's father from Maine. Earl is alive, this man is reading his name off a list. "Are you sure? Do you know him? Do you know who he is?" I cried. "Have you talked to him? Earl is fairly new to the company." The voice says his name is on the list, but what does that mean? "How can you be sure? When will I know for sure?" I see a glimmer of hope but I can't be sure. There could be a mix-up. I will keep praying and then a half hour later I hear Earl's voice. He is still in the city, and the call only lasts a few minutes, but it is him. We told each other "I love you" and he promised that he would be home as soon as humanly possible. He wanted to know that the kids were safe and then the line went dead.

Naturally, a wave of relief spread throughout my body like the hot sun in the summer. I almost could not believe the miracle of Earl's survival. My first thought was to thank God, for he had answered my prayers. He was faithful! I hoped and prayed that many other people would also be so lucky, but in my heart I knew that not everyone would be. It was a disaster like we in the U.S. had not seen before. "Hurry up and wait" suddenly and thankfully had become the new order of the day. What else was there to do? Earl had no idea when he would be home. I had so much to be grateful for, but I was still scared knowing he wasn't home yet. All transportation was shut down to and from the city, with only emergency vehicles allowed to go in and out. It was not at all safe. I needed to see and touch his face to know for sure he was okay but he wasn't going to be home any time soon. He had to make his way home most likely on foot. While I have never actually been into New York City itself, I did grow up and work in Los Angeles, and I could imagine what it would be like to walk home all those miles. Somehow I had to figure out what to do with myself in the hours before Earl returned home in order not to go completely crazy on the craziest day of my life.

The phone rang again and it is Cameron, my oldest at Junior High. I realized instantly when I heard his voice that I had forgotten to call his school, to make sure communication was shut down and the children would not be exposed to the mornings horrific events. How could I forget to check? Mommy guilt flooded over me. "Is Dad dead?" he whispered. Oh my God, no child should ever have to mouth those words.

Into what kind of horror movie have I put my kids? Thankfully I had just talked to Earl, or I don't know how I would have answered this horrifying question from my 11-year-old. "No, Cam", I said, "No, I have just talked to him and he is fine. He is coming home as soon as he can." "Are you sure, tell me the truth Mom, I have to know the truth." Cameron says. I try to reassure him by telling him I have heard his Dad's voice, and I know he is okay but he still has to get home safely. "It could take all day, so you need to stay at school. Are you okay to stay at school?" I ask. I suspected that the phone would be going crazy all day, and there would possibly be bad news about people Earl worked with or others he knew. I wasn't strong enough to deal with it and didn't want my kids to see me break down. I needed time to process the day and pull myself together. It ripped me apart not having them close by on such a scary day, but I was trying to shield them from some of the horror. Being in New Jersey and not right near New York City, I felt they were safe at school, but if they were at home they would have been exposed to all the raw emotion flowing in our house.

By now it is past noon, and the phone has started to ring off the hook with nearly continuous calls from family and friends out on the West Coast. Back home on Bainbridge Island, several people had gathered at a good friend's house as soon as they heard the news. They sent their kids off to school and waited and prayed together for word on Earl's welfare. Eventually, after we spoke, several of the schools on the Island made an announcement over their PA systems that "Coach

Earl" had made it out of the building and he was okay. The horror had spread to the west coast just like that. Another friend who lived next door had been riding the ferry to work in Seattle, when they turned the boat around and told everyone to stay out of the city if possible. Dozens of calls from family and friends reached me with their love and support pouring through the phone lines. One of Earl's friends whom he has known since elementary school called to check on me. He knew Earl worked in downtown Manhattan but did not remember exactly where. I will never forget the dead silence on the phone when I told him Earl had been in one of the buildings. I cannot even remember the number of people who called and offered to come and help, almost begging for something, anything, to do, to help. I could feel their emotions and desire and need for instructions, but I was incapable of making any decisions. Earl and I had done nothing but make decisions, one after another for the last year, and now none of them was working out as planned. I knew that we would have to make many more in the days to come, but I truly believed that I wouldn't be up to it. I had no confidence left in my ability to be rational or decisive. I was so grateful that Earl is alive and yet so overwhelmed with the idea that nobody in the world will ever feel safe again. That the term "safety" has left our lives and our kids' lives forever. The world has changed forever this morning and not for the good. It reminds me of the first time you lose a loved one, or when you understand the meaning of divorce; you are permanently changed.

I remember trying to reach my brother who was on a plane out of San Francisco. I was terrified that the killing was not over and that more planes would go down and more lives would be lost. "Will anyone be able to fly safely in a plane again?" I wondered. Many of the people I talked to that day told me how they felt scared beyond anything they had yet experienced in their lives. The attacks brought to all of us the laser focused reality of life's fragility; and how they feared it would be the last time we talked. I remember that everyone was emotionally open, raw and bleeding. It was like swimming in a sea of emotions. Some never having been felt before; some of it was beautiful and amazing; and some were too terrifying to consider. I imagined it felt like what it would have been like to be at my own funeral. The compassion I felt for the other families was threatening to swallow me up. The guilt and empathy was overwhelming, and I wasn't at all sure I would ever be able to not feel like this. I questioned why my family was so lucky and wondered how all those other families were going to survive their loss. I don't remember not crying, as it seemed like a constant stream for hours, only I did not feel any better from the tears. I feared I would never be able to stop, never be able to feel happy again, with so much pain in the world.

Somehow the hours passed, and finally it was four o'clock and my kids were due home on the school bus. I questioned how would I explain this to them when I could not understand it myself, and on top of that, I still did not know when Earl would be home. I was still terrified that something could happen and he would not make it home safely. I remember telling myself that I must pull myself together and be a parent and somehow show strength that I did not have. I ushered them off the bus and into the house and explained to them that while the World Trade Center buildings had been hit by planes, Dad was okay. I muted the television and let them watch the image of the planes and the building collapse once, and that was it. I don't think they saw the images again for months. I told them Dad was coming home, and they could talk to him on the phone when he called but it could take hours. I let them go outside and play but told them that it would be good to pray for the people in New York and Washington, D.C. and Pennsylvania. I knew Cameron was struggling, but as the oldest he instinctively knew he had to try and set a good example. He had borne the brunt of my children's trauma when after being identified as a student with a parent who worked in the Trade Center, he was called to the school office earlier in the morning to make that difficult phone call. Now, after almost eight hours of debilitating stress, I simply waited, and the phone never stopped ringing.

CHAPTER 7

Reunited

Departing Manhattan

It wasn't long after the North Tower fell that we were told to evacuate the city, as word had spread street by street, business by business. A group of us, the exact number I don't recall, headed out and made our way to the Westside Highway and then north toward midtown Manhattan. There was a steady stream of other people headed the same way, and eventually we learned that boats from the local tourist cruise fleet were ferrying people back across the Hudson to New Jersey. Some of those in our little group lived in the city, and at one point we parted company, as those who lived across the river sought to find a ride. It wasn't hard to know where to go; we needed only to look for the long line of people seeking the same thing. We queued up and spent more than an hour, possibly two, in the now hot, mid-day sun, shuffling slowly forward, up and down a pier, as we made our way to the front of the line and our turn to board the next available boat. Every now and then I would gaze south toward the billowing clouds of smoke that poured from the collapsed ruins of the Towers. At some point, I recalled a conversation I had with my boss shortly after joining the firm. When I asked him why he chose the Trade Center location, particularly in light of the 1993 bombing, he had replied quickly and confidently that lightening never strikes twice. In hindsight, the fact that both attacks were not due to nature but rather inspired and carried out by man, was of little consolation.

I want to pause here and describe for you my emotional state at this time, as well as provide a sense of what it was like to witness all that was happening around us. First and foremost, it was impossible to shake the feeling of fear as the enormity of what had happened began to sink in, and the laser-like focus on just getting out of the building gave way to a broader, more inclusive sense of what was going on around us. From the constant stream of first responders and their equipment pouring down the Westside Highway toward the billowing smoke; to the tents and trailers that I soon learned were makeshift morgues used in mass casualty events; and the sound of full throttle military jets overhead, circling Manhattan, all lent an all-too-real sense that we were at the origin of something that may not yet be over.

As a group, we had walked in both silence and sporadic attempts at normal conversation. No one seemed to have the focus or desire to engage in much real interaction. Short bursts would be followed by longer silences. I recall someone asking me how I liked working in New York now, and I actually laughed and answered something to the effect that it was nice while it lasted. While not a conscious thought at the time, I think I knew deep down that I would not be coming back anytime soon. I so wanted to just be home with Arlene and the kids. "God, please just let me get home quickly," I prayed. I didn't know how much longer I could keep it together, so I turned inward and asked repeatedly for His help to give me strength.

Hoboken to Bayonne

Once across the Hudson River, it became apparent that all transportation services and systems had been shut down: no trains, no highway traffic, no nothing. So we walked. With five or six of us left in our group, we headed south to Jersey City, where one of the fellows had his condo and car, which he used to ferry us further south to a parking lot where two of the others had left their cars that morning. Fortunately, they had their car keys and I caught a ride to Bayonne. Eventually, I wound up that afternoon at Bayonne High School and a temporary Red Cross shelter that had been set up there. I was given food and a place to rest. Alone now for the first time since before the attack, I found a quiet corner of the gym and began to cry.

The overwhelming magnitude of the day's events had finally taken their toll, and all the emotions I had pushed back over the course of the day simply came rushing to the surface. I recall a profound sense of loss, not only for the thousands lost today, but for their families and children. My own emptiness poured out of me as I struggled to cope with the fact that I felt trapped and unable to get home where I knew I needed to be, and where I suspected Arlene needed me to be as well. I asked God to help me. Everything I had tried to accomplish with the move east had come crashing down with those Towers today. I had nothing left to give in terms of energy or ideas. I only knew I needed to get to Freehold and be with all that really mattered to me in this crazy world. "Oh my God, what if I had died today?" This was the first occurrence of that thought and I wept with both guilt and thanks for God's gift to me. My body shook as I gave in to the enormity of what He provided me and denied so many that day.

Over the next several hours, I was able to call Arlene multiple times to touch base and just let her know I was okay and trying to solve the transportation problem of how to get home the remaining forty or so miles. Later that afternoon, I moved from the gym back outside to sit in the warm sun. I spoke with several people about my day and theirs and where I needed to go. Someone tapped me on the shoulder; it was an officer with the Bayonne Police Department who told me he had overheard me say where I lived and that it wasn't far from his home. He told me to stay put and that he would come and get me when he was relieved from his shift. He didn't know what time that would be, given all that was going on, but he reiterated that I was not to leave, that he would come back and find me and take me home. And so he did. It was around 7 p.m. that evening and we headed out to the New Jersey Turnpike, which was completely void of traffic, having been shut down except for emergency vehicles in the area. He was a wonderful man and was very concerned about me and my need to get home to my family. We rode most of the way in silence, and I suspect his instincts told him how much I needed just that. I am embarrassed to say that I don't know his name, but I will make you readers a promise to try to find him on my first visit back to Ground Zero. We pulled into my driveway; I turned and thanked him with a handshake and tearful eyes, as I stepped from the co-pilot seat of his unit. Our eyes met once again as he saw me wave goodbye. "Thank you," I mouthed, and he was gone.

Home at Last

It was around eight o'clock and I heard the sweetest sound: Cameron yelling "Dad! Dad's home!" He had seen the patrol cruiser stop and let me out while he was playing catch with a couple of the neighbor kids. As I headed for the garage door of our house, Arlene, Alex and Noelle ran out and all joined Cam in mobbing me for hugs, kisses and more hugs. I can't recall if others were present or not, for all I could see was my family. I headed straight for the door and entered the house with everyone right by my side.

The first thing I remember about the next several hours is how Arlene and I seemed to have the same instinct and approach to dealing with the day's events, my homecoming and the children. We down played any danger discussions and kept reinforcing the fact that Dad was home now and that everything was going to be okay. They were only 12, 9 and 7, and our parental protection radar was apparently operating on the same frequency and with similar amounts of power. We talked about the fact that while our country had been attacked today, as they had seen on TV while waiting for me to get home, I was home now and in one piece. Before long it was the usual, "How's everybody's homework situation?" and "Who needs to take a bath before bed?" Throughout this time, Arlene and I would exchange glances and nods, confirming for each other the strategy we both naturally pursued. I think we both instinctively knew that neither one of us wanted to open the door to further emotional trauma today, especially any involving the kids. We both knew we were spent, and didn't want the children to know just how upset and close to the line of losing emotional control we truly were.

Once the kids were tucked in and said their prayers, Arlene and I sat down with a couple of drinks and just started to talk. First about how much we loved each other and then about what we had each been through and how we couldn't believe that this had happened to us on top of everything else. "It wasn't my time," I kept telling her. She cried and told me about all the phone calls and how she and others had prayed for me. I then realized that I needed to call my parents and sister and some of our close friends back in the northwest. This was both easy and difficult for me, as I wanted to let those concerned know that I was all right, but I had trouble making small talk, as most of me just wanted to sit quietly and not think too much. I guess I was experiencing a delayed kind of shock, as it felt better to just do nothing.

After all the phone calls were finished, we watched the news constantly, as I had not seen any of the day's incredible footage. It was very late when we finally turned in. Arlene fell asleep first, as I worked the remote control from my side of the bed. I can't remember falling asleep that night, but I must have at some point, as I recall waking on Wednesday morning to the sound of the kids having breakfast and getting ready for the school bus with Arlene. Nothing sounded more normal than that. For a brief moment before I gained full consciousness, it was as if yesterday never happened. It was the perfect start to the first day of the rest of my life.

Ten Days

Over the next several days, Arlene and I tried to maintain as normal a schedule and environment as we could in a house full of cardboard, lost have–to-haves, and generally way too much disorganized post-move-stuff. We even managed to go out to dinner and a movie on our 16th anniversary that Friday, September 14th. Cam's birthday was coming up the next week, and Arlene was working hard to plan something and, of course, to have the shopping done.

As far as work was concerned, my job was not mission critical to the firm's day-to-day operations, as my team and I were building a new product capability. I received word to take as much time as was needed and didn't go in until sometime the week of September 17th, when a company-wide grief counseling session had been scheduled. It was great to see everyone at the firm's emergency backup office site in Jersey City and to find support for one another. I still miss some of these wonderful people dearly. It was, however, evident to me for the first time consciously that I felt like an outsider, and I began to realize that I just didn't have the strength to carry out my family's master relocation plan any longer. After all that had happened, I really only wanted to go home, back to Bainbridge Island, and to leave all this madness behind.

That evening, I began in earnest my efforts to make my desire a reality. What would I do, though? The reason we were here in the first place was that I couldn't find a job back home. One call to a great friend, an older-brother-I never-had type of friend, changed all that. He had been both an investor in Deposit Software and a long-term mentor. This one call would ultimately solve everything. He connected several dots like only he can do, and over the next several days or so, all the pieces fit together, providing me a real solution. By Friday night, September 21st, I now had the power to choose whether to stay or go home. While still certain it was the right choice to head home to Bainbridge Island, when to let Arlene know it was a real option was something I was, for some reason, unsure about. But not for long.

CHAPTER 8

Going Home

The Decision

As previously mentioned, Arlene had been experiencing an increasing amount of allergic and or stress-related eye irritation ever since we arrived in New Jersey. Sometime during the second week post 9-11, one of our neighbors kindly provided her with a referral to a local specialist. Arlene secured an appointment for the following Saturday, the 22nd of September. That morning, she headed out for the doctor's office but returned after only about thirty or forty minutes. I was standing at the door near the kitchen, looking out into the garage, when she stepped out of the car. I saw right away that she was crying and upset. As we met, she sobbed that she couldn't find the doctor's office, and she was so miserable. And then I knew. I knew it was time to go home. Back to Bainbridge Island and our house and family and friends. Back to all things familiar. I asked her, "Do you want to go home?" And she stopped sobbing and looked up at me with unbelieving, pleading eyes. The kind of look we all have had when we really want something so badly, yet don't really believe that it will come true. "Really?" She said. "Yes, really," I responded. "Right now, today," I added with a smile. "Really?!" she now screamed at me. "Yes, let's call the kids in and tell them. We've got some packing to do!" I yelled back at her joyful smile. We were jumping up and down like kids. And so, when we called Cameron, Alex and Noelle to join us in the family room and shared the same question I had just asked their mother, we all wound up jumping up and down on each other, laughing, smiling and crying all at the same time. The decision was made. We were going home.

Road Trip!! Again

Over the course of the next three hours, all five of us ran around in a frenzy trying to pack the Suburban with everything we deemed essential for life on the road and back at home until the moving van could redeliver the full complement of Johnson family worldly possessions. We have come to remember the double, cross-country move of 2001 as a really bad vacation that we took way too much stuff on. Everyone pitched in, and we had the car loaded and ready to roll by

2 p.m. Even Chucky the cat seemed to understand where we were headed as he eagerly sought a comfortable spot to lounge among the duffel bags and suitcases. Everyone piled in, and we headed for the New Jersey Turnpike and points west. As we passed through the town center of Freehold, I saw the Fire Station with its makeshift memorial outside the open bay doors. I couldn't help but offer a silent prayer of thanks and wonder if any firefighters from here had been lost.

As we made our way into the Pennsylvania countryside on Interstate 70, the kids settled in to watch a movie or play XBox on the small TV we had originally rigged for the trip out to the east coast. It all seemed a little unbelievable still, and didn't really register with me until we had passed the first one hundred miles and I needed to stop and fill the tank. It was the familiarity of filling the big tank on the Suburban that made me focus on the fact that the next time I would need to do this would be three or four hundred miles down the road. How quickly and easily it was to make things better, I thought. Just sit back, steer and let the wheels roll on.

The Pennsylvania segment offered several opportunities to travel through tunnels under the rolling hills. Each time, the sun's rays were waiting for us as we emerged from the darkness. Arlene and I noticed together and expressed to each other the sensation of a weight being lifted off our shoulders. It was as if God was waiting for us and shining His light to guide and protect our journey. At some point in the early evening when we stopped for a bite to eat, I told everyone that I was feeling good and very awake and wanted to drive all night. Without question or concern for an actual bed to sleep in, they all said, "Let's go for it." And so we did.

It's hard to say much in detail about the next forty-eight hours or so. Time seemed to fly in tandem with the miles as the wheels of our Suburban rolled westward. Overall, our route back to Bainbridge Island was identical to the one we had just traversed in late August. For some strange reason, though, everyone seemed so much happier; I can't imagine why! At some point, one of the kids began to cheer each time we entered one state and departed another. Soon we were all cheering. I know we all enjoyed the feeling of one more down, fewer to go. This little ritual took place regardless of the time, day or night. From New Jersey to Pennsylvania, Pennsylvania to West Virginia, through to Ohio and on to Indiana, Illinois, and Iowa, we cheered each one. I pulled in for a six hour nap at the Missouri River as we entered South Dakota, and then resumed through Wyoming and on to Montana, the Idaho panhandle and finally our Washington. We passed through Spokane, crossed over the Cascade Mountains, and descended down to the Puget Sound basin and beautiful Bainbridge Island. All told, I figure we crossed the country in about 54 hours of actual driving over a 60-hour period of time: two and one-half days!! I don't know what the record is, but I can't imagine doing it like that ever again. Only the unique set of our circumstances created the perfect mix of adrenalin and will to complete the journey in such a short time frame. I was seeking safety and the comfort and love of friends, family, and community for myself and for my family. It was our salvation, and it was waiting for us when we arrived at our house on Bainbridge Island, between four and five in the morning on Tuesday September 25th 2001, just two short weeks after 9-11.

CHAPTER 9

Settling Back In

Home Sweet Home

Sometime before noon, our friends began to call or stop by and welcome us home. This was truly something Arlene and I will never forget. Our local fire department's motto is "Neighbor Helping Neighbor," reflecting its history with deep tap roots of local resident volunteers. Without being asked, our friends had filled our kitchen, prepared for our children's sleep and comfort with beds and couches, and generally brought anything they could spare to make life more bearable until the moving truck could return from New Jersey with our belongings. Imagine the look on our faces when we pulled in early that morning of the 25th, went in our house and found all of their preparations. Balloons, flowers and "welcome home" signs adorned the kitchen. It was really an awesome sight! What friends, what wonderful friends we have! This truly is our home and where we belong. Nothing has ever felt so right before. I know Arlene and I have thanked God for them many times, but it never really seems to be enough. So much of our happiness here, in this community called Bainbridge Island, is because of them. We both thank you all from the bottom of our hearts.

Thursday the 27th was the kids' first day back in their old schools and, needless to say, something they were so excited to do. They, too, have many friends and found comfort back in their midst. Bainbridge schools are fantastic and the staff exceptional. Many helped in ways of which I'm sure we were never aware, but all displayed the utmost care and understanding of the trauma my family had just experienced. By the end of the week, this part of our lives seemed to really be back to normal.

During the next day or so, I contacted my friend who had been caring for my malamute, Shadow, and made arrangements to pick him up. I was so happy to be reunited with my fuzzy old friend. He seemed to be happy too, but we would need to deal with a lingering depression he seemed to slide into after a couple of weeks. The cure? Another Malamute of course! A puppy no less, and what a pistol. Sabrina, now a little over three years old, turned out to be just what the doctor ordered. Her arrival had the double benefit of providing my daughter, Noelle, with a puppy to care for and play with, as she had been mourning the permanent loss of her golden retriever Molly. It wasn't fair to the family that had adopted Molly before our move to think they should return her, and Noelle came to understand and accept that thinking with the help of endless licks and frolicking on the floor with Sabrina.

Back to Work

My duties at my new firm, Seattle Northwest Securities, didn't start until around the first of October and I still needed to fly back east and meet the movers to pack and load our belongings and then drive my Camaro cross-country one last time. The department I worked in was headquartered in the company's Portland, Oregon, office; and while I would be assigned to work out of the Seattle office, it was expected and understood that I would spend significant amounts of time every other week down in Portland. It's really not that far, especially when you compare it to the cross country road trip I had become all too familiar with. I could leave the house on Bainbridge at around 4 a.m., traverse the Olympic peninsula to Olympia, where I would catch I-5 for the straight run south across the Columbia River and into downtown Portland. Door-to-door, it was a little over three and one-half hours. I typically would go for two nights and spend three solid days with the traders and product managers in an effort to get up to speed with both how they ran their businesses and what my role would actually look like.

My office in Seattle was located on the forty-third floor in central downtown, surrounded by other buildings of equal or greater height. Parking was available in a typical multi-level facility beneath the building, and I must confess to having frequent fears about being both underground and also at near landing pattern eye level with the aircraft approaching Seattle-Tacoma International Airport from the north. I tired hard those first months not to let my fear get the better of me, but I was still having recurring nightmares, and it often took a brief trip down to ground level and a quick walk around the block to settle my nerves.

Over the ensuing three-plus years since 9-11, this effect has thankfully faded and I'm sure that my opportunity to join the Bainbridge Island office of RBC Dain Rauscher in May of 2003 is in no small part responsible. Our building is only two stories tall and my office has a window that opens, a nearby balcony and an unbelievable view of Eagle Harbor, the Seattle skyline, and the Cascade mountain range. It is a wonderful place to work with great people, and small enough to feel like a family. Best of all, it's on the Island and requires less than a ten minute commute. For this I am very thankful, as the time I used to spend commuting to Portland and Seattle can now be spent coaching, attending the kids school activities and generally being more involved in my community.

One More Time!

The moving company had given us the dates of October fifth through the seventh of 2001 as the pack-and-load time frame for the return trip west. I made arrangements to fly one-way to New Jersey to meet them and essentially clean up any details, grab my Camaro, and get the hell out of Dodge. The flight back east for me was a real struggle, as I was not happy about having to fly back into what for me was a dark nightmare. I don't recall much of the uneventful flight, other than they seemed to run out of Jack Daniels somewhere over the Rockies, and I thankfully caught a short nap. Once on the ground, I took a cab out to Freehold and began preparing for the packing crew due to arrive the next day.

At some point the next morning, I called our landlord, a wonderful woman whom I had only met once, and let her know both the fact of, and reason for our forth coming departure and my desire to negotiate an exit from our one year lease. She basically said, "What's to negotiate?" and proceeded to tear up the lease and then wished me and my family God's blessings. I thanked her profusely and told her I would never forget her generosity and graciousness. With that not insignificant detail resolved, I went about taking care of the rest of the items on my to-do list: visit the kids schools and return books; rent a truck and ferry everything out of the storage unit back to the house; shut off the phone and other utilities; close out the bank accounts; grab pizza's for the packers; and anything else that needed my attention. These couple of days went by in a flash and before I knew it, I was settling into my Camaro again, having watched the moving van disappear down the street. It was around 6 p.m. and while I knew I wouldn't be pulling any all night driving sessions by myself, I figured a good six or eight hours on the road would put me well on my way back home and into a fourth cross-country road trip. I won't bore you with yet another recap of a cross country drive except to say that I did stop at Mount Rushmore once again and loaded up on a great shirt made to look like the star' and stripes. I had been asked the previous week, while at home, to speak about my experience to my home church congregation, Christ Memorial in Poulsbo, and I thought the pastoral staff would love these shirts.

I did make a detour off the usual I-90 route in western Montana that would allow me to swing south through southern Idaho and visit my parents and sister in Boise. This stop was pretty emotional as it was the first time my folks had seen me in about six months. With moving, progressive health problems and now my 9-11 experience, Mom and Dad were a little frazzled. I stayed overnight and late into the next day just talking and sharing our experience with them. While no one said anything, I think the idea of moving them back to the Seattle area was in the back of my mind. After all, if I could move back, why couldn't they? That is, in fact, what eventually occurred in the summer of 2003.

Moving On

I made it home to Bainbridge on the 13th of October, one
day ahead of the moving van. It was great to be home again,
even though the next couple of weeks would be filled with
the huge task of unpacking. Neither Arlene nor I nor the kids
seemed to mind, as we were just so thankful and happy to be
back. Days quickly turned into weeks and weeks into
months, and soon it was Thanksgiving, Christmas and then,
of course, the New Year, 2002. For me, the holiday season
that year delivered a special gift. I haven't spoken of this before
but it was the fact that we had Christmas right where we had
it the previous year, and not where we had expected to have it
in 2001, that brought me my first real sense of closure on my
family's hideous experiences of 2001. With this came a much
deeper sense of awareness and appreciation regarding my own
good fortune and ability to put my family's life back together.
So many families this year would be unable to do this. I knew
then that while the passage of time would provide its natural
healing, part of me was going to be forever driven to never
forget those lost that day and the pain and suffering their families would continue to bear far into the future. How could I
forget, when each day, in fact each breath, was something my
family and I had that they did not. More and more, I found
myself asking for God's help to understand this.

Later that year, with the approaching one-year anniversary
of September 11th , I was asked to speak about my ordeal

that day to several groups. One was organized by a group of churches, including ours, in the neighboring town of Poulsbo and was held in the local high school gymnasium. It was very emotional for both me and the audience, but it provided me with a new insight into the importance of my witness regarding the day's events that previous September. I became aware of the almost healing-like power my words had on some who listened. Perhaps in some way, those here on the west coast needed to feel closer to that day, and I was right there for them to see and hear and even touch. Another opportunity to speak was at a 9-11 memorial service at the Bainbridge Island City Hall, organized by the city and local fire and police departments. It was situated outside on a glorious, sunny, blue sky day exactly like the one we were remembering from one year earlier. A huge American flag was flown over the podium, suspended from the extended arm of a ladder truck. Someone told me afterward that a lone eagle had circled directly overhead during my speech. A final opportunity that day occurred at my daughter's school where the Principal had organized a memorial service and all the children gathered on the play field to form a giant circle by holding hands. This was a powerful reality for me, as it was impossible to escape the recognition that our children's generation had witnessed, at a very young age, something no other generation ever had; an attack at home, on American soil.

These three events on the first anniversary marked a new beginning for me. I already had a strong sense that this was important to talk about for myself, but I had not yet come to understand or even fully realize the link between the need of others to experience that day through my eyes and my own personal healing. This self discovery is at the heart of my efforts to write this book and to find new audiences that may be helped by hearing the story of an ordinary family during extraordinary times.

CHAPTER 10

Speaking Out

Throughout much of my career in the banking and brokerage worlds, I often found myself speaking in front of a group of people. Sometimes it would be to a senior group of executives like a Board of Directors or Executive Management committee and other times to a sales force. I have addressed convention-sized crowds, participated on panel type break-out sessions and, of course, made thousands of pitches for the product, service, relationship or cause that was my focus and topic at any given time. All of these taken together have provided me with a measure of confidence that in turn provides a sense of comfort when standing up in front of groups of all types and sizes. This chapter is the closest thing in this book that represents my life presently and as such, is and will, God willing, remain a work in progress for many years to come. At its focal point is the realization that I now hold so dear; that September 11, 2001, will remain a life-long passion driven by the need and resulting desire to share my experience with others in the hope that in my story, they will find something that touches them personally which they can use in a positive way to live a fuller, richer life and to never take anything or anyone for granted.

First Responders

One of the best things to take place in my life over the past three years was the inquiry several close friends made to me regarding my interest and willingness to run for public office as one of three Fire Commissioners for the Bainbridge Island Fire Department. It didn't take me very long to agree, as I felt extremely honored to be asked and given the opportunity to serve, in even a small way, with this community of heroes. Not unlike a corporation's Board of Directors, the Commissioners are both the public's and the Department members' focal point for overall business decisions that encompass everything from strategic direction, to spending authorization, to tax policy, to labor negotiations. I have learned a great deal during the first eighteen months of my six-year term, but nothing compares to the many new friendships I have found and the ever increasing appreciation I have discovered through a new awareness of the internal workings of the Fire Service and the men and women who choose this most noble of careers. God

Bless all of them, here on Bainbridge Island and everywhere else in the world, where First Responders stand ready while the rest of us go about our daily lives. I encourage everyone to get to know some of these people. Go and visit a local Fire Station, take your children, participate in local community events sponsored by them. They are after all, neighbors helping neighbors.

Many opportunities to speak about my 9-11 experience have resulted from this association with the Fire Department. In particular, one of the men responsible for my participation is a medic with the Seattle Fire Department. He is a giant of a man, standing over 6' 7," but with both a gentle heart and skilled hands capable of caring for the smallest and weakest among us. I recall our friendship really took root when, during a school fund-raising event, he offered up for auction what is called a "ride-a-long." This is a twenty-four hour shift whereby you go with a Medic 1 unit and its two-person crew and experience a day in their working lives. Now, I don't want to embarrass my good friend so I won't go into to much detail, but suffice it to say I got into a bidding war with the school principal, who by the way is a woman, over this auction item. It probably wasn't a fair contest, as I was driven by my experience to make sure I came out on top, and I did. What an experience! Over the course of twenty-four hours, I watched these heroes bring back a heroin-overdosed twenty-something from the dead, team up with a complement of firefighters to rescue an injured teenager from a precarious rope swing accident, treat and transport numerous individuals from injured bicyclists to the elderly in nursing homes, all with the ultimate in professionalism and compassion. But the best was enjoying a fabulous steak dinner at the firehouse, and getting the chance to tell these men and women about my experience from 9-11 and what I witnessed from their east coast brethren that day in terms of bravery, courage and compassion in the face of extreme personal danger. Over the past three years, I have had the opportunity to repeat this at various times when my friend has been assigned to different stations throughout Seattle. Each time I have grown more convinced that my story and message is something they not only want to hear, but need to hear.

In the Community

Outside of the first responder community, my early speaking efforts have taken me to several other types of groups, namely local Rotary and Kiwanis gatherings. These organizations are a huge part of the fabric of our society in America and serve to act as a similar type of "first responder" when it comes to the needs of their communities that are not being met either directly or completely by various arms of local governments. While I have not personally belonged to this type of organization, I feel a kindred spirit towards them as their members are all volunteers, putting in their time, sweat and dollars to make their communities and the lives of their neighbors better. I have addressed a dozen or more of these groups in and around the Kitsap peninsula over the past three years and look forward to meeting many more in the years ahead. The people that choose to sacrifice and make others' needs their own are unique and special. I find great satisfaction in communicating to them that their efforts, while not carrying the same level of personal or physical risk as those who came to rescue me that day, are nonetheless aligned in spirit with them and provide great comfort to thousands of their fellow citizens each and every day.

Another part of our community that has provided me with the opportunity to tell my story are various churches and religious groups, including faith-based private schools. I enjoy these talks greatly, as I always seem to feel a little closer to my God when given the opportunity to share my witness under His roof. In the course of writing this book, I became aware that other survivors have taken their experiences and put them to pen as well, albeit with a much more focused perspective on God and their faith. I mention this most certainly not to criticize, but to simply contrast and explain my belief and approach. This effort for me, while having a religious component, is not first and foremost a religious mission or message. Instead, I find that in speaking out, I am helping to create and spread a greater awareness of, and appreciation for, the members of our society who choose to serve, and this of course includes the men and women who wear the uniforms of the armed services of the United States of America. I believe in God, I am a Christian and as such, believe that Jesus Christ

is my personal Lord and Savior, but that is not why I wanted
to write this book or why, I suspect, you are reading it.

In the Classroom

At other times, I have been asked to address school children
ranging from fifth and sixth graders to young adults in a high
school environment. These opportunities are both hugely
rewarding to me, yet at the same time can be a real challenge.
There was a TV show years ago called "Kids Will Say the
Darnedest Things." How true that is! Some of the most difficult questions have come from youngsters struggling to
understand, while trying to create their own perspective or
sense of what 9-11 means. Being part of that process for them
is my reward and something I take very seriously. Our children,
this current generation of American youth, had to witness the
reality of a world changing from pre-9-11 to post-9-11 and is
something no other generation of children has had to cope
with. Not even Pearl Harbor brought the reality of the world
as a dangerous place so close and real to the children of the
1940s as did the attacks on the Twin Towers and the Pentagon
to the children of this generation. It is of paramount importance to their future, and therefore, the Nation's future that
they come to understand the significance of that day.

Perhaps my most memorable experience to date has been
the opportunity and privilege to address first the football team
and, later, the entire student body of Kamiak High School in

Mukilteo, Washington north of Seattle. I was introduced to their head football coach through a gentleman who happened to be an assistant coach there and who had heard me speak at a breakfast meeting of a local Rotary club in nearby Kingston. Each year in late summer prior to school starting, this coach organizes a retreat-style camp for his coaching staff and players. In the process of setting the particulars of time and location, we spoke on the phone, and I knew right away that this was a man I would want to know better. Having played high school sports, including football, myself, and coaching my own boys' teams over the years, I believe I know a leader and a winner when I see and hear one, and this coach has both of these qualities in spades.

The day of the event was a drizzly, gray unusual August summer day, and after watching the team workout and the coaches in action, I really knew I had found a special opportunity. The degree of professionalism, discipline, work ethic and winning attitude displayed by this team and its coaching staff was both impressive and infectious. I found myself thinking several times the old "Put me in, coach," as I was motivated just watching. That evening in a log style, open air campground shelter where I enjoyed a meal and made new friends, I offered my story to eager ears and open hearts. I learned that several of the players had parents or other close relatives that were either firefighters or U.S. military personnel, some on active duty and away from home. The best moment of the evening came during the question and answer portion at the end when I called on one of the players.

He was in the back row, and had been next to or right in front of, one of the coach's wives who also had near shoulder length blond hair. I brainlessly addressed him with a "Yes Ma'am?" and the room exploded in hysterical laughter. The coach was standing with me in the front of the group by the large stone fireplace, and we had to hold each other up, we were laughing so hard. Afterwards, I made it a point to find this young man and again offer my apologies. We laughed and hugged, and I learned that his father was an executive officer aboard the carrier Abraham Lincoln, the very ship that my medic friend and I had welcomed back from the Persian Gulf the year before in May of 2003. We had taken my seventeen-foot Boston Whaler and a huge American flag tied to a makeshift mast out into Puget Sound and cruised right alongside the huge ship and her escorts. What a small world.

My other experience with Kamiak High School came on Veterans Day in 2004. My coach friend organizes this effort every year, and what an event! I was blown away by the full orchestra and singing chorale, numbering over one-hundred-and-fifty students, as they played and sang songs like "The Battle Hymn of the Republic" and "God Bless America." Their gymnasium was packed to the rafters as this 4A school has seen significant growth in recent years with the build up of the Everett Naval Base. Many students have military family members, both past and present, and the patriotism I witnessed was very moving.

In the days following this event, I took the time to reflect back on what I had just experienced and participated in.

Something was bothering me, and I wanted to identify what it was, and deal with it. After some significant soul searching amid quiet reflection, I came to realize that what was bothering me was the inescapable fact that my beloved home town and alma- mater, Bainbridge Island High School, would not only be unlikely to ever host such a patriotic celebration, but that the vast majority of my neighbors would be, more likely than not, diametrically opposed to the very idea. This reality, while something I had long ago come to accept, and live with daily, had been brought once again to the forefront of my mind with my visit to Kamiak. The division in my heart between home-town and home-land had been made crystal clear once again. I was forced with having to accept the fact that in spite of my experience, and my resulting desire to speak out in support of our country's efforts in the War on Terror, that this was something most of my neighbors simply disagreed with. No amount of effort on my part will likely ever change that, and I think it was this realization that weighed heavily on my heart and mind.

In the Future

I must say that over the last year, speaking out has become more than something I just look forward to doing. It is something I find myself actively seeking more and more. Perhaps the process of writing this book has been a catalyst for what may in fact, turn out to be a significant opportunity.

Regardless of any commercial success that may result from this book, I have come to understand that my story has the potential to offer those who hear it a variety of benefits, not the least of which is an opportunity to discover or reacquaint themselves with the goodness and basic humanity that can reside in each of us. In order to broaden my speaking opportunities, I have developed a handful of concepts or themes that can be driven and magnified by one or more of the core messages embodied in my experience. These would include concepts like "Obstacles or Opportunities" or how we choose to look at and respond to the curveballs that life throws our way. Several applications of this primary theme would address situations of change in our work or personal lives whether anticipated or simply thrust upon us. Another theme would entail "Embracing Adversity" and how the need to develop early in life a set of key skills that can empower us to achieve a level of success in life that most people can only dream about.

I don't know how far or in what direction my efforts to speak out will take me, but I am excited and anxious to discover them. One personal goal I have set for myself is to help establish September 11th as a National holiday. The memory of those lost and the absolute need of future generations to never forget demands nothing less.

CHAPTER 11

Have You Forgotten?

Those three simple words, "Have You Forgotten?" were immortalized in the aftermath of 9-11 by two talented and patriotic musician-songwriters, Darryl Worley and Wynn Varble, in their beautiful work bearing that title. During the course of researching and drafting this book, I needed to learn about the process of gaining legal permission to quote copyrighted material such as song lyrics. I can report my success by providing in print, with permission, Darryl and Wynn's powerful words to you.

> *I hear people saying we don't need this war*
> *I say there's some things worth fighting for*
> *What about our freedom and this piece of ground*
> *We didn't get to keep 'em by backing down*

They say we don't realize the mess we're getting in
Before you start your preaching
Let me ask you this my friend

Have your forgotten how it felt that day
To see your homeland under fire
And her people blown away?
Have you forgotten when those towers fell?
We had neighbors still inside
Going through a living hell
And you say we shouldn't worry 'bout Bin Laden
Have you forgotten?

They took all the footage off my T.V.
Said it's too disturbing for you and me
It'll just breed anger that's what the experts say
If it was up to me I'd show it every day
Some say this country's just out looking for a fight
After 9-11 man I'd have to say that's right.

Have your forgotten how it felt that day
To see your homeland under fire
And her people blown away?
Have you forgotten when those towers fell?
We had neighbors still inside
Going through a living hell
And you vowed you'd get the ones behind Bin Laden
Have you forgotten?

I've been there with the soldiers
Who've gone away to war
And you can bet that they remember
Just what they're fighting for.

Have you forgotten all the people killed?
Some went down like heroes in that Pennsylvania field
Have you forgotten about our Pentagon?
All the loved ones that we lost
And those left to carry on
Don't you tell me not to worry 'bout Bin Laden
Have you forgotten?
Have you forgotten?
Have you forgotten?

I can recall exactly when I first heard their song over the radio in April 2003. I was driving back to Bainbridge Island from Portland, Oregon, following an overnight business trip. It was after dark and the traffic on Interstate 5 northbound was fairly light. That's a good thing, because I began to cry, and then sob, and then finally cry out in anguish. I pulled over on the right shoulder and set the parking brake with the motor still running, while my tears flowed and my heart raced as this emotional tsunami washed over me. I remember sitting quietly after the song was finished as I turned off the radio. I didn't want to hear anything else; except that song. These words had hit me like a locomotive. The rest of the three-hour drive home was spent in silence as I processed my feelings and the reality of the physical reaction that had just occurred. It is something that happens still to this day, but now thankfully with much less outward emotion and instead a strong sense of purpose and renewal and determination to be a voice for the expression of the words in this song title, and a reminder to all, welcome or not, that I will never forget.

It was several days later when I found myself near our local mall and music store. They had the CD in stock, and after purchasing it, I returned to my car only to face the fact that I didn't yet have a CD player in my stock 1994 Camaro. I have a special place at home which I call the Roadhouse, a detached two-car garage that serves as an automotive shop for my car projects, a second home to my poker buddies on Friday night every other month, and my personal sanctuary. It is a place where I can have a fire in the wood stove, listen to the radio or play CDs, and have my two Alaskan Malamutes in to warm up or dry out. This is where my thoughts and emotions become clearer, more focused and better soothed. There have been many Saturday mornings since I first heard "Have You Forgotten?" when I try to relive that moment in an effort to provide an emphatic "NO" to the imperative question that song title forms. It is in this place that I have found my ability to best think about the life-changing event that 9-11 was and still is for my family, myself and our country. Sometimes it is a mourning; sometimes a celebration. But it is always thankful: thankful to God for delivering me that day; thankful

to the community of first responders and their ultimate sacrifice; thankful that once again our country finds itself blessed
with the right leader at the right time. And yes, I understand
that after reading that last sentence some will now close this
book and discard it with the household trash, but I hope you
don't. I hope those who disagree with that assessment will still
read on.

At the beginning of my efforts to organize my thoughts
regarding the scope and content of this chapter, I came to the
inescapable reality that this part of my message would have
the potential to divide rather than unite. It could backfire and
serve to harden the already deep division that so recently was
bright red and blue on our living room TV set. Then again,
my purpose in writing this book is to tell my story, and I
would be lying to myself and you the reader if I tried to gloss
over the fact that I believe 9-11 and our country's response
will be seen from the clarity of history as one of the greatest
voluntary sacrifices one nation has ever given to the world.
The stakes couldn't be higher. With success comes the
freedom and awakening of tens of millions of our fellow man
to the reality of an existence driven by the individual's ability to
celebrate life, liberty and the pursuit of happiness: key concepts
that seem to escape so many caught up in our present day
sophistication and comfort. Failure, on the other hand, will reap
untold misery and hardship. Not just for those who will remain
enslaved through ignorance, fear and allegiance to leaders whose
stated objectives are the destruction of America and all she stands
for, but for our own children and grandchildren who will be left

to face a hostile world which will have witnessed the limit of America's power and influence to create a better future for all mankind. That is not a world any of us should like to see. A world where the hope of those not free is extinguished, smothered under a blanket of darkness which man has always seemed so ready and willing to spread over his fellow man.

No, I have not forgotten. Have you?

For more books and
more information visit:

www.stairwelltoheaven.com